FROM ZERO TO HERO

DANIEL DELATOUR

Order this book online at www.trafford.com
or email orders@trafford.com

Most Trafford titles are also available at major online book retailers.

Print information available on the last page.

ISBN: 978-1-4907-5985-2 (sc)
ISBN: 978-1-4907-5977-7 (e)

Trafford rev. 07/07/2015

www.trafford.com

North America & international
toll-free: 1 888 232 4444 (USA & Canada)
fax: 812 355 4082

CONTENTS

GRATITUDE LETTER

I want to start off by thanking the people that helped in the publication of this book. First of all my mother, Marie-Jude Delatour, who was my number one supporter and believed in me since day one when I told her that I had the brilliant idea to write a book. Even though she knew that I didn't like to read nor write, she still supported me and pushed me towards accomplishing this dream. Second of all I would like to thank Melissa Rose Charles for putting the incessant idea of me being a motivational speaker in my head until I actually listened to her and worked towards that goal. All of this would have never happened if you never came into my life and that I am truly grateful for. Third of all I would like to thank Hedyeh Yahyaei for granting me some of her precious time to be the first person to review the book in the most critical way. What you did means more to me than words can actually describe. I can never truly repay all of you for what you have done for me. Last but not least I want to also thank all the people who told me that I could not do this and also those who told me that this was a stupid idea and a waste of time for you have been my biggest inspiration to actually finish the book, pour my soul into it and turn my vision into a reality in order to prove to you that when you truly want something and that you are willing to put in the work and effort required, you can do it. There are many other people that I would like to thank. I apologize for not naming them here. I thank you all for the impact you had on the creation of this book. It would not be what it is now without you. Thank you for all the support that you have brought to this project. I truly hope that you enjoy reading it as much as I enjoyed writing it.

GRATITUDE LETTER

INTRODUCTION

I have decided recently that I wanted to make a difference not only in my life but also in the lives of people surrounding me. We all dream of success in our lives. Most of us want to be able to buy the most expensive things in this world and show our riches. We think that happiness can be achieved only by doing so. It is the "American Dream" to be happy and successful. We unfortunately associate happiness and success with money, assuming that these riches (happiness) can only be bought with money. One of the most common mistakes that we make as human beings is to keep thinking that when we have money we will be happy and our lives will be extraordinary. It is important for you to realize that money does not ensure happiness. The perfect way to illustrate this would be to use a quote from Democritus stating that "happiness resides not in possessions and not in gold; the feeling of happiness dwells in the soul".

It is important to focus on everything in your life besides the monetary currency that your country uses. What happens when you focus on different aspects of your life, without thinking of the financial implications, is simply unbelievable. Unfortunately, I cannot explain what happens or how you will feel when true happiness will be present. It is something that you have to experience for yourself since everyone has a unique reaction to it. You need to understand that nobody wants the exact same thing as you. Therefore, that means that no one will live their happiness the same way you do. Each individual will feel different emotions and react in their own way.

With this said, this book is here to highlight some key stepping stones that will help you achieve your true happiness. Fair warning on this concept of happiness : remember that true happiness cannot be achieved overnight. It is a learning process in which you will gradually discover who you are and what you particularly like. Only then can you be happy, for you will be doing what you enjoy doing the most.

We will address multiple subjects that are necessary for you to follow step by step thus allowing you to get closer to your <u>personal</u> happiness. It is imperative that you take each new step with a great deal of conviction and thirst for knowledge and maintain a level of focus while going through them without skipping any of them. Each of them has a role to play in helping you figure out the path that you will need to create to get to that overwhelming sense of happiness.

Let me tell you a secret. It is imperative that this be said now because this is the key to unlocking your true potential and starting your journey with all the right tools. First you need to define your own success. As stated before, in this society, we define success by the size of our bank accounts or the assets that we own. Therefore, if you are financially rich, you should be happy. In other societies, your success is define be the number of children you might have. Regardless of what the status quo of your society is telling you that you need to possess to be happy, I am sorry, yet relieved, to tell you that money or any other physical asset has never and will never bring true profound happiness. You could have all the money in the world and still be miserable to the point that the poorest human on this planet would pity you. Why is that? How can somebody that has so much money, a house to dream for and so much more be so miserable? That is a very complicated question which requires great thinking when answering. The answer is that <u>they to do not have what they truly want in life</u>. Like stated before not everyone wants the same things therefore not everyone wants financial riches beyond their wildest dreams. We have to define success as Christopher Morley did.

Morley said that "there is only one success, and that is to be able to spend your life in your own way". In simpler terms, if being successful for you means spending time with your family and you are able to achieve that goal, then, at that point, you have achieved your vision of success. If your dream is to grow the biggest botanical garden known to mankind and you are capable of fulfilling that dream then you are successful.

The key here is to realize that only <u>you</u> can define your own success. Know what <u>you</u> truly want in this life. Now that the key to your success has been revealed, the following chapters will guide you through your process step by step, to provide you the knowledge that will help you achieve the goals that you have set out for yourself.

Remember that the journey you are about to start is not easy. In fact, if it were easy then everybody would do it or would have already reached it. I need you to really commit to this and make sure that you give it your all. Whatever you goal may be, you need to make sure that at the end of that journey, you are capable of telling yourself without a doubt that there is nothing else you could have done to make this dream of yours become a reality. If you can do that, then let us work on the following steps. You will need to perfect them one after the other in order to be where you need and want to be. It is important that you realize that these steps are not independent from one another; each and every one of them will influence the others in various ways. If you can master each and every one of them then there is nothing that you cannot do in this life. You will be able to have anything you want.

It is one if my biggest dreams that the knowledge that I will share with you, helps you accomplish what you set out to do. It will be one of my greatest accomplishments to know that I have, in this way, changed people's lives not only for the best but also to teach how to accomplish their vision by making it a reality. I know that with these empowering notions, you will be able to build your life around the values that you have chosen. Take the concepts that I am sharing with you, review it and assess which of those points will prove to be useful for your personal pursuit.

CHAPTER 1

IDEA

I am going to do something that is really unusual but necessary. I have to ask you a question that will be the foundation of your quest. I know it might seem odd to start off with a question but I need you to be honest with yourself and answer the following question: <u>What do you want</u>? The first step to your personal journey is to determine what you really want. You need to unsure that the pillars of your life are set strong. One of those pillars is the initial idea of your goal and what it truly represents to you. What do you truly want to succeed in? In this stage, I need you to sit down, relax and think of everything you like to do in life. It could be something small like playing an instrument or reading a book or listening to music, but it is important that you do what you want to do. I strongly believe that if you sit down and calm your mind, you will be able to <u>reflect</u> on your unique tastes in regards to the wonders that life has to offer and you will be able to figure out what your special talent is.

I believe that everybody has at least one special talent that they know of. We have a spectre of wonderful talents that we never use. Most of us don't even know that we possess said talents. To figure it out you need to be in a state of relaxation and become one with yourself. Some of the ways to do this would be for example, when you are listening to music, close your eyes and truly listen to the words or listen to each individual instruments that are being <u>carefully</u> played by each player with great passion. When someone plays an instrument with passion, you can feel the expression of that passion in their music. They always make sure to hit the desired notes at the desired moment to ensure that the desired sounds come out as clearly as possible. If you prefer listening to nature and recognize all its beauties, I would suggest that you close your eyes and listen to all the birds singing in harmony. I am positive that by now you are probably wondering why we are focusing so much on closing our eyes. I have realised that when we close our eyes, our perception of the world with our other senses magnifies and intensifies our experience. This will permit us to truly analyze and appreciate what we are experiencing in a whole new way.

Our eyes trick us in many ways. They make us focus on what's obvious and thus we lose sight of the true beauty that surrounds us daily. We rely so much on our eyes that we tend to forget to focus on the beauties of nature. By closing your eyes, you focus on the universe and unconsciously start to feel the natural flow of life. This flow will help you relax, and help you focus on the subtleties that surround you. These subtleties are, as impressive as it may sound, a part of each of us for we will all experience them differently. The way I will feel in regards to the wind brushing against my skin will not be the same feeling for anyone else on this planet for I am the one experiencing it while using my sensitive motors. We input a lot of our experiences in our feelings thus they are exclusive to us. If you understand the concept I just explained, you will be able to study yourself a little more every single day and you will be able to find out what you like. Now, knowing what you like is only the stepping stone to the immense power of the universe. Once you figure out who you are and what you like, you will find yourself in a position of continuous desire to do said activity because that is what brings you true profound joy. As time will go by, with the peace of mind that you will experience, you will start getting ideas to multiply and perfect the things you like doing. The number of times you do things you enjoy doing will only bring you more pleasure and help you advance intellectually on your personal growth. Therefore if you like biking then you will get new ideas on how you can go out and bike more. In other words you will think of new ways to make biking more interesting for you. This important key concept of "time" will be explained in greater detail in two different chapters. The reason I have to develop this concept in two different time period is due to the fact that I believe that the idea I will introduce in the second segment will truly be understood following the presentation of some other theories that I will have you work on. Time will be one of the most important if not life changing keys that you will get to learn to appreciate through this book when planning/changing your life.

As stated above, now that you have figured out what you like, with more practice of said activity, you will want to make it better, more interesting for you and therefore you will try to input your own personal style to it so that you can enjoy it even more. What you just went through with that reflection, is what I like to call a "life changing idea". One of my favorite authors Les Brown said that "you only get only two to three extraordinary ideas per year that have the potential to drastically change your life". The question that I need you to ask yourself is : <u>what will you make of those ideas</u>?

Remember the initial idea that you got from your relaxed and happy state of mind! If you desire to keep that personal state of mind, you will have to make a choice. The first choice is the positive one. Go forward and work on said idea to make sure that your happiness lives on so that you could live your life the way you want it. The second one is the one I hope you avoid. You let that chance pass you by. By doing so you will be forced to live a life of mediocrity because you did not want to put in the necessary work. If you are reading this, I already know something about you that maybe you might not know about yourself. Without you knowing, by picking up this book and reading it, I know for a fact that you have made the decision to start living your life the way you wanted to because you want to live a self-driven life doing the things that you want to do. I can already tell you that you are on the right path to making sure that your happiness grows and multiplies. You have at this very moment taken the first step in your spiritual [1] process. With the following key points that I have carefully chosen to share with you, you will see yourself achieving a level of spirituality that complements your happiness to accentuate your senses on the vast beauties of this life. Once you figure out what you want to do, you will need to work on it day in and day out to make it happen. Prove to yourself that further down the line your spiritual happiness is reached. Let's go through the different stages of the life changing idea that you decided to act upon that will force you to grow in ways you have never envisioned.

---

[1]   Spirituality: When we talk of spirituality here we are talking about being one with ourselves. Do not mix spirituality to religion. Religion may bring a certain level of spirituality but the contrary is not necessarily true.

CHAPTER 2

THE PLANNING STAGE

It is very important that you to take this step as seriously as possible. In this planning stage, I need you to be very fastidious. From what I have learned throughout my own endeavors, this is the biggest building block that you could have. Consider this as the second stone you are setting that will take you to the beginning of your personal path. The first stone being the initial idea that you had to find, you now need to know what you need to do to get to your end goal. The key to succeeding in this stage is to write everything down while you are working on your dream goal.

I do not believe that there is such a thing as a bad idea. Every idea, if given the chance, can become something tremendous with the right amount of work. Just write down what comes through your mind regardless of how "stupid" [2] it might seem to you. Remember that nothing is truly stupid. <u>You</u> thought about it so it can work for you if <u>you</u> take it seriously. Write everything that you may need, regardless of what it may be. For example, if you need a tricycle to make your dreams a reality, then write down the fact that a tricycle is needed.

Once you finish writing down everything that you think you might need, it will be the time to write the draft of your action plan. This action plan will be the explicit representation of the steps that you think you will need to take during this process. Before anything, I want you to know that in regards to the two steps that I just presented to you, you will have to come back to these once in a while during your process to make some changes. The changes can go from adding more steps or more items that you think you may need, to removing some items or steps that you realized you might not need after all. It could even be just moving them around.

---

[2] Stupid: I put stupid in brackets here because I do not believe that something could be stupid.

Let me give you a small trick in regards to removing items on your list which I unfortunately had to learn from my mistakes. When removing an item on your list (especially if you made your list in an electronic format) just cross it out. Never completely erase it because the beauty here is that maybe further down the line, that thing that you deleted might become useful. Unfortunately since you deleted it then you might not remember it when called for. However, if you just cross it out, you might find use for it later on when you review that draft item list. If you are writing that list on physical paper, the same process applies. Just put a thin straight line on the item that you want to "eliminate" [3].

Now comes the decision that you need to make. Pay close attention here because this is the second part of the planning stage. Once you believe that your first draft is "good enough" [4], I need you to be honest and true to yourself, for you will need to make a decision. Make a vow that you will take all the necessary decision to make this dream become a reality. Whatever decision you need to take, you must promise yourself that you will take it. Whatever road you have to go through, promise yourself that you will do it. This is one of the hardest things to do because most people will be afraid to go get what they want.

Here is a trick that I learned on my path and that I still use regardless the situation I have to face. Les Brown said "You can either live your dreams or live your fears". I personally interpret this quote the following way but it is understandable if you interpret it differently. As long as it works for you that is all that matters to me. For me, this quote means that you need to decide that you will live your dreams regardless of what might happen instead of living your fears. Here is the astonishing philosophy that I got from that quote which I keep reminding myself every day: Whether you live you fears or you live your dreams you will be doing what you want to do. Therefore why not strive to do what you really want to do? That which will make you happy. One thing is for sure, if you do live your fears, all your doubts and insecurities will be justified and you will never be happy with your life. You might be content but never happy. I will present a deeper and more thorough explanation of this mindset in a future chapter. If you have made the decision to follow your dreams and not live your fears, the following chapter is for you. What you will learn in that chapter will be one of the most important key notes that will be necessary and is at the same time unfortunately unavoidable to every living being.

---

[3]   Eliminate: Very important to not take this word lightly. It is very powerful and can have negative repercussions if used in a wrong way.

[4]   Good enough: I have to apologize in advance for this term. I want you to know here that I used this word because I had no other choice. I need to illustrate the fact that your draft will never be perfect but it can be modified to your liking throughout the whole process.

CHAPTER 3

TIME

There are two ways to analyse the concept of time. I will explain both concepts in great detail to you throughout this chapter. You need to understand that your time is the most precious resource that you have on this earth. You must realize here that I intentional said "<u>YOUR</u>" time because for me, anybody else's time is irrelevant just like for you anybody else's time should be irrelevant. Time is something that everybody has and yet never really possesses it.

Let me explain : time is that type of resource that once it is gone, you cannot get it back, therefore you never truly have it. When you think you have it, at this very moment, you lose it at the same time. During the time it takes you to evaluate how much time you have, seconds are already flying away. You are thus losing so much time at this very moment.

Let me illustrate this in another way: if you lose money, you can win it back or work to gain it again. It is possible to get the amount that you lost or even more. If you lose any material possession, then you can go out and buy the same product or something fairly similar. This cannot be applied with time, for once it is gone, once you lose that second, you cannot get it back. Once your day is done, you cannot go back in time and re-live that day. Even now, the time that I am using to write this book, I will never get it back for I decided to use it for this particular activity and I can never go back and change what I did during that time. That is one way of understanding the concept of time which implies that whatever work you put in at this very moment, you need to make sure that it is worth your valuable and irreplaceable time. With this been said, you really need to think of the task that you are undertaking in that moment and ask yourself if it is truly worth your time.

Now the second notion of time that you need to understand very carefully is that it is a very limited resource. In other words, no one never has and will never know how much time is available to them to do anything. This is in correlation with the first aspect in various ways. The first aspect focuses mainly on the quality of the act whereas here, we are focusing mainly on the numerical representation of said time. A good trick that most successful people use is quantifying said time which helps them understand this theory in the following way. People will tell you that you have all the time in the world to do whatever you want therefore, why not just relax and have fun for now? You will have time to work on your dreams later so just enjoy life for the moment. What I am saying to you and what most successful people will say as well is that you should enjoy life by working on your dreams right now.

Think of it this way, you only have today to work on your dreams because you do not know if you will wake up tomorrow. Some people push it even further by saying that you don't know if you will be here in the next hour therefore every second that is given to you should be used effectively for pursuing your dreams. Successful people will use this concept on a day to day basis and they will not fritter their time doing meaningless activities that will not take them where they want to be. They prefer investing all the time and effort that they have on that one dream. They believe in it, that is why they want to materialize it. Since they do not know if they will be present a day from now, they put all there energy on that task right now thus, at the end of that day, when they finally get the chance to rest[5], they know that they gave it their all. They know that there wasn't anything else that they could have done during that time to get them where they wanted to be. Now, since we know that everybody gets a maximum of 24 hours in a day, I need you to go over your day before you rest and think about every single action[6] that you took throughout your day and see if it was worth it. After this, take it to a whole new level and eliminate for future references any actions that you think were unworthy of your time. If you were drinking and partying too much and it doesn't get you closer to your dreams, then stop. If you felt like you stayed home and watched television for too long yet you planned to go to the gym, then don't turn on the television anymore. Force yourself to get up and go to the gym as you had planned. Think of the concept and apply it to this situation. You will not get back any of the time you have spent watching television instead of going to the gym, therefore you just lost your chance of getting stronger and healthier.

---

[5] Rest: make sure here that like most successful people, you earn this. This word refers to replenishing energy that was used in a specific activity so make sure that the activity that you are undergoing is worthy enough for you to rest later.

[6] Action: remember that the absence of an action is in fact an action in itself.

Bruce Lee said "If you love life, don't waste time, for time is what life is made up of." If you can do this for every action that you took in a day and eliminate those that were unworthy of your time, then you will be able to make the right choices if you get another 24 hour set of time. The more you will eliminate the frivolous actions, you will have no other choice but to replace them with good actions that are worthy of the limited time that you have.

I also want to advise you to take some time to reflect on where you are in your steps along your journey. Sometimes rest days are necessary and the time you take to reflect on your actions is just as valuable because if you do not make time to review your actions, you will never be able to determine which ones you want to keep or eliminate. Just make sure that it is not time wasted as an excuse to not take an action because like I said before, the lack of action is also an action. This brings us to our next chapter that will help you decide which actions are worthy or not. You need to decide this based on your situation and goals. Only then will the time be used effectively.

CHAPTER 4

ACTION

This is the easiest thing to do and yet the hardest. This falls in the category of easier said than done. In this step, I need you take serious action to make your dreams come true. Correlate this step greatly to the previous one. The actions that are required will need to be taken in the shortest possible time. You need to be aware of the fact that you might not be the only one that got that one idea that you are pursuing at this very moment. That is why I need you to take all the actions at the necessary moments. Whatever the actions required, I need you to not waste time and go for it now because if you do not do it now someone else will do it in your place and you will regret it sooner or later. Think about this, I have heard so many people in my life say : "why didn't I think of that?" or "That was my idea, I <u>could have</u> been rich by now". So many people have ideas but never act on them and then regret when they see someone else that had the guts to follow those ideas become rich, famous and successful. On a personal note, in my life, the way I figured out what actions where necessary, was by actually following the path less travelled. Do the things others are not willing to do in order to get the things that they will not get.

Let me explain this: like I stated before, most people will only do what is necessary to "survive" [7]. I am telling you right now that you don't want to be that type of person. Do not follow a path that is pre-made. I need you to create your own path. The perfect example to this is to think of a forest that you want to explore. You don't explore a forest by going down a path that someone else made. The person that created the path before, followed <u>his</u> or <u>her</u> path

---

[7] Survive: I used this term here to refer to only doing the necessary things to stay alive. Eat, sleep therefore only living for no specific reason that will make you happy.

by creating it one step at a time which would later allow you to follow their footstep. I need you to create your own path by cutting down all the problems you will encounter along the way. Regardless of the situation that will present itself, you need to stay strong while keeping your grounds and facing each problem that life will throw at you. A very famous quote from Rocky states that:

> *"The world is not all sunshine and rainbows. It's a very mean and nasty place and I don't care how tough you are, it will beat you to your knees and keep you there permanently if you let it. You, me or nobody is going to hit as hard as life but it is not about how hard you hit. It's about how hard you can get hit and keep moving forward, how much you can take and keep moving forward. That's how wining is done. Now if you know what you are worth then you have to go and get what you are worth but you have to be willing to take the hits."*

What he means by this is that you need to keep moving forward. Life will try to punch you and knock you out cold. What you need to do is take every single punch and, no matter what, keep moving forward. Eventually, you will be where you want to be regardless what your specific dream is. If you work hard enough at it and give it all you got, you will achieve greatness. I want you to remember that if it were easy, everyone would do it. But it is also true that when there is a will, there is a way.

Since you now know that you will get punched, let me share something with you that helped me get through each and every punch that I received from life. If you win, you will be happy, but if you lose, you will be wise. What I learned from this was that when life hits you, if you are capable of taking those punches, you will be happy since you are now one step closer to your dreams because you were strong enough to get hit and keep moving. Now here is the tricky part. When you do get hit by life and you fall hard, you need to remember that you are now wiser because you found a way that shows you that what you are trying to accomplish won't work. Now since you are wiser, you will need to get back up and try again. If you can pass this difficult situation, you will be one step closer to your dreams as well but if you keep getting hit over and over again, you will eventually make it happen because with each punch you get stronger and wiser. It took Thomas Edison more than 1000 tries before his light bulb finally worked. I am telling you that you need to keep getting hit until something good comes out of it. Each small goal that you will accomplish will bring you tremendous satisfaction. If small goals bring so much satisfaction, imagine how much satisfaction you will feel once you have achieved a bigger goal.

Take the path less travelled that will lead you to an astonishing amount of failures and problems that you will have to deal with because life will for sure punch you and try to knock you out but I need you to stay strong and keep moving forward towards your goals. The end goal is worth those punches. The beauty of this is that after some time, you will develop some habits that will be immensely helpful along the way.

CHAPTER 5

HABITS

In the last chapter we talked about taking serious, continuous actions to turn your dreams into reality. This chapter is focused on the effects and results of those specific actions. When you take the decision to do something either good or bad, you will unconsciously develop habits that gravitates around that specific action. Habits are going to be a great asset when you start your path to your dream. It is important though that you realize that you need to build good habits that will help you. Avoid the bad habits as much as possible.

Habits will push you forward and challenge you as they are required to. Since you know that there are good and bad habits, I need you to choose the right actions that will develop the right habits which will eventually help you get closer to your dream every single day. I know for a fact that a habit is hard to develop and even harder to maintain. The beauty about it though is that once that habit is in place, it is hard to get rid of it. Think about this deeply. It is hard to get rid of a habit. Ponder upon it and imagine the immense consequences of developing the bad habits that only demoralize you anytime and every time they can. Imagine how hard it will be to pick yourself back up after getting hit by all the problems that you will have to face.

Here is a trick: you cannot afford not to be you. So I need you to get back up and go against those bad habits. Keep on making the right decisions without being afraid to fail. Tell yourself that you cannot fall back in those bad habits. I need you to fight as hard as you can and eventually, you will be able to break those bad habits and replace them with good habits that will strengthen you and give you the energy to create more good habits. Since you have less bad habits now, you will have more energy to fight the other bad habits and knock them down. This creates the cycle presented earlier of creating better good habits. Create that wonderful fulfilling cycle of destruction of bad habits and replace them with good habits that will push you closer to your dreams.

Jim Rohn said "First we form habits, then they form us". Since they form us, might as well get formed by the good ones. Be healthier and become faster and smarter in avoiding certain problems because you have learned how to fix them and eventually you will even be able to avoid certain problems. Here is a trick that I learned very quickly when I was working on developing my good habits. A proverb that I like a lot states that "a wise man learns by the mistakes of others, a fool by his own". I was offended when I first heard that saying but then when I reflected upon it, I analysed it while supressing my pride. I finally realised that the quote was really saying that it is faster to learn from the mistakes of others and avoid falling for the same mistakes as well. Since I witnessed the negative results that those actions brought, I should try to avoid them. It doesn't mean that you will not make mistakes nor that you are a fool for making your own mistake. On the contrary it is impossible for you not to make mistakes. What this quote is saying though is that you need to look at other peoples failures and learn from that. You will then be able to perfect your habit and your actions and go farther than the other person. Look at someone in your entourage who has failed at some point and you will need to learn from that failure. Use their failures as guidelines because they went through it and succeeded. The knowledge they have acquired and are now sharing with you will help you avoid making the same mistakes. Keep moving forward until you reach the point where your dreams become reality.

The second part of the quote is fairly subtle. It is important to learn from those people who have failed, you will have to associate with them at some point. But guess what, they got where they are because they learned something that you might not know yet. Therefore they are fairly wiser than you on that specific subject or situation. By associating with wise people, you will become wiser and you might in return give them some wisdom as well. You will push yourselves with each other's energy every single time. Let me give you an example of this. If you go to the gym alone and you are doing something wrong, how will you ever know that it was wrong? Now, if you go to the gym with a partner, he will be able to tell you what you are doing wrong and therefore you will have the opportunity to perfect your technique. Plus when you go to the gym alone and you fail at an exercise, you will maybe get one more push in and be done. The difference of having the partner there with you lies in the fact that the partner will push you beyond your limits and make sure that you get in two or three more repetitions thus forcing your muscles to go beyond their limits so they can grow later on.

Now that you understand the importance of habits, let's talk about the results that these good habits will bring to your life.

CHAPTER 6

MOTIVATION/DETERMINATION

If you follow through and keep your good habits, you will find yourself in a place where your motivation is boosted up as a result of those previously mentioned habits. With more motivation, you will be more determined to pursue your dreams every single day by applying those habits day by day.

Here is an important fact that you need to be aware of. We as humans are extremely lazy. Think of the society in which we are currently living in where we are trying to invent so many different gadgets to make our lives easier. We try so hard to reduce the amount of work and effort that we have to put into certain tasks. Once again you need to avoid being your own enemy and force yourself to install those habits so you can find the motivation to keep going and achieve your dreams.

Let's analyze this and see what we can get from it. Most of us usually say I wish I could … (fill in the blank). It could be that you wish you could own a business, or you wish you could be an amazing father. Whatever you want to achieve, I want you to stop for a moment and think of the difference between would and could. When you use the word would, you are talking about the imaginary portion of that situation. Therefore you are imagining what would happen if you would be a business owner. It mentally requires more energy to leave that imaginary realm and bring your dreams to reality. You will need to work hard to start visualizing the end result of said dream for it to become a reality. On the other hand, when you use the word could, you automatically imply that you can do the task that is presented to you. You already know subconsciously that you can ……………………..(fill in the blank). For example : Would I be a good husband? You do not know if you would or not. But if that phrase were to be changed to: could I be a good husband? Subconsciously you are starting to reassess the situation and already thinking of what defines a good husband to then compare to your way of doing things.

Understand that when you change the word would for could on a daily basis, you are already motivating yourself to start the process and get yourself on the right track. You will start evaluating your actions with other people's actions and see if you can learn anything from any of the mistakes that they made. You will be more determined to make that "could" become a reality because in your mind you already thought of the multiple paths and actions that will help you achieve that dream. What this will do is give you a boost of energy and reinforce your beliefs. You will make yourself stronger every day because you kept saying that you could do it.

I will share with you a new point to this concept that I have found during my hard times. I realized that you need to always do what you are afraid of doing. By understanding the difference between would and could, I figured out that the same does not apply to can and will. What I found in regards to "can" is that you are just telling yourself that you can do it but there is no explicit engagement to said action. You are merely expressing the possibility that the power to accomplish this action is in you. What this does is that it gives you reassurance that it could be possible. You know what you need to do to make this a reality but you did not convince yourself to do it and therefore you might not take any actions.

This is where the concept of "will" comes in place. "Will" automatically starts the planning process which means that you are telling yourself that you will take this challenge and face the difficulties that will present themselves to you. When you use "will", it forces on you the obligation to undertake this action sooner or later. Now do not mistake this with the absolute truth that the action will become real. There is a big danger with this concept. The danger is that it is kept in the future permanently if we do not bring it in the present. The final stage to motivating yourself comes in the combination of those concepts. Since you can do it and you told yourself that you will do it, now I need you to "<u>DO</u>" it. You already know it is possible and you have already decided that you would go through it. Why do we not take it upon ourselves to make sure that the definitions of both concepts become reality?

This new enlightenment will push you to a new mystical realm that will help you get ahead if you embrace it with open arms. You are now IN the process which means that you can say: "I am doing it". Not only do you know that it is possible, but it is possible for <u>you</u> and you are taking the actions therefore do not tell yourself "<u>I will do it</u>" but rather "<u>I am doing it</u>". When you enter that realm, you will begin to feel a strong power flow in you. I need you to just listen to that power and accept it. I will unravel the nature of this mystical realm when the time comes so as to ensure that you take the knowledge with all the essential tools for major success in achieving your dream. For now I just need you to trust it and embrace it the best you can to tap into its wonders and its infinite powers.

CHAPTER 7

WHY

One of the previously mentioned tools that is primordial to your success is to discover your why. It might seem weird to express this theory in these terms but bear with me and let me explain. The definition given to understand your why comes from a very famous motivational speaker named Eric Thomas. He defines "why" as being the reason behind your actions. You will need to define your "why" this very moment if you have not done so yet. Keep in mind that your "why" must mean the world to you. Your "why" has to be something that you would do anything for. Your "why" can be anything from making a difference in the world to somebody like your loving mother or your father, your exceptional wife or family or it could even be to help other people have a better life. Whatever it is, it has to be important for you because your why will be present on your road to success. My "why" is to make a difference in this world. I want to help people reach their goals and dreams. My biggest "why" is to support my wife and my family financially to give them the opportunity to live their lives fully without the stress that comes with financial obligations. I deeply want to be able to change my family's life for the best.

It might seem useless now but let me share with you a small quote that will make you understand the power that this "why" contains. Friedrich Nietzsche says : "He who has a "why" to live can bear almost any how". In other words, when you have a "why", regardless of the difficulties that life will put in front of you that may try to knock you down, by remembering your "why", it will help you get back up and challenge each and every problems that will try to knock you out until you beat them to the floor and go to the next level. For example, remember that for me, if I don't give up now and I keep writing this book, the sales will help me receive a certain income that will help me reach financial freedom faster. I will therefore be able to provide a better life for my family. By pushing through, I can guarantee that you will see results if you work hard enough and take it seriously. Another example would be that, if my "why" would be to inspire people to be healthier, then if I keep pushing myself to my personal limits [8] when I'm at the gym, I will become stronger and therefore I'll feel happier and healthier. Eventually, I might be strong enough to become someone's inspiration and motivate them to become healthier.

You need that push. That is where the power of your "why" resides. It will be your fuel to keep you running towards your dreams until you catch up to those dreams and you grab them and say: you now belong to me. Here is the tricky part, as much as your "why" will motivate you to keep on pushing forward, it also needs energy. You have to understand that you need to feed your "why" as well. Here is how you do that: You need to make sure that your "why" is your greatest motivator. By being your greatest motivator, this ensures that your "why" stays encaged in your head and cannot escape. If you encage it, you have to feed it and it feeds off of your personal emotions and desires. If you are always thinking about it, then it will push you to give all that you can to succeed in your journey. The more you think about it, the more it will push you and the more it pushes you, the closer you will be to your success. Fortunately, the closer you are to your success, the stronger and the more important your "why" will be for you. It is a spectacular cycle that is always to your advantage so therefore feed from it and feed it so that you can succeed.

It is possible that at some point, you will become discouraged. When that happens, remember your "why". Feed from that energy and push on because you know how important this is to you. Once you feed from that positive energy and you put up a fight against the obstacle that life just sent towards you, your "why" will feed from your thoughts and force you to fight back against a specific obstacle. Once you get through that obstacle, your "why" will push you towards another one and then another and another until you reach your goal.

When I was younger, I saw the Rocky Balboa movies and in one of them, Sylvester Stallone playing Rocky Balboa gave this speech to his son. That speech got to me and I have since then tried my best to model my life around it. It is one of the best examples that can be given in regards to having a "why" in your life. He said:

> "You, me or nobody is going to hit as hard as life. But it is not about how hard you hit, it's about how hard you can get hit and keep moving forward, how much you can take AND KEEP MOVING FORWARD. That's how winning is done."

---

8   Limits: the beauty of limits is that they can be surpassed and therefore new limits are always created.

Therefore you need to keep moving forward and only one thing can help you achieve that, your "why". To get to where you want to be, you might not have somebody there to help you which means that you need to help yourself and use the cycle that was presented earlier to your advantage. Use it to your advantage and develop your reason to keep going. Rocky said "regardless of the number of times that life will punch you and beat you to your knees, we need you to get back up and keep fighting back" over and over again until you make it happen. After hearing that speech, I told myself that I would always get back up and keep taking the hits. I know that eventually, I will be fast enough to start dodging those hit, then I will be strong enough to block them. In the end, I will get stronger with time and I will start fighting back and in turn, hit life back again and again.

The great Frank Sinatra said it best. He said : "the best revenge is massive success". So when life strikes you down, get back up, achieve your goals and succeed for that will be one of the biggest punches you will ever be able to give life.

It might seem very unfair that you only have your "why" to help you out in such a huge fight against life itself. Even though your "why" is strong enough to help you win this fight, it never hurts to have some additional help. I want to warn you right away that this help might need a lot of work before it is fully available to you. In the next chapter, we will focus on developing the necessary skills and mindset that will create that additional help and afterwards improve their strength to make sure that you succeed even when the situation seems dire and that you want to quit. With the next steps that will be presented to you, and if you really take this seriously, life will not be able to put up a good enough fight to pin you to the ground and force you there. You will be strong enough to get back up and put up a serious fight.

CHAPTER 8

VALUES / STANDARDS

I cannot even find the right words to illustrate how important this chapter is on the road to achieving your personal goals. It is crucial that you set yourself a set of values that you WILL follow. I also suggest that you combine some high standards to those values to ensure that you reach their highest worth.

There is a very famous quote from Les Brown that says : "reach for the moon, if you miss at least you will lend on a star". When you put everything together to make sure that you have an advantage in order to succeed, then even if you fail, you will win so much during your time on the road. Not only did you learn so much from your failures, but you also might have positively changed the lives of 5 people instead of 10 which is in itself a victory. What's important here is to see the positive side that you introduced to someone. Even if it was only a single person's life that you changed for the best than you still accomplished something for I can guarantee the person will be grateful for this new vision that you gave them. Now, you just need to get back up and keep pushing until you reach your goal.

I would like to add something more to that quote and say that once you land on a star, then you are only OH SO FAR away from the moon. In other words, you have less of a distance to travel from that said star to the moon. In that case get back up and try again. Most people will feel very discouraged for not reaching their goals on the first try but I am telling you that you need to start being conscious of the immense power that is stored in you and I need you to define your personal value.

I am here to tell you that you are priceless. There is nothing in this world that is worth more than you. Nor is there anyone that is equal to you. You are unique and therefore you should define and acknowledge your worth. In the last chapter, I talked to you about your "why" and I gave you a quote from Rocky. Now I want to share with you the second part of that quote that is in direct correlation to your personal value:

"If you know what you are worth then go out there and get what you are worth but you have to be willing to take the hits and not point any fingers saying that you are not where you want to be because of him or her or anybody."

Here, he is referring to your personal value. How much do you think you are worth? Once you can figure that out, then go after it and do not let anything stop you along the way. Let me give you an example, at your current job, if you think that the position that you are in right now is the place you should be at this point in your life, then you should be happy. If by any chance you feel that you deserve more, then go after what you think you deserve.

Unfortunately for you, I am at this very moment telling you that you are worth more than your own perception of yourself. You will always be the worst judge of your personal life. You will always be the one that will undervalue your specific actions. You are your worst and biggest critic. I need you to be conscious of this and tell yourself that you have no other choice but to keep on pushing.

If you don't go after what you think you should get, then it will be entirely your fault when you do not get what you wanted. To get it, you would have to put in the time and energy into it. You only have yourself to blame if you do not succeed. You cannot blame the government for it is only here to do what it is intended of doing based on the laws and regulations that are currently in place. You cannot blame your parents for they have given you all that they could. Even if they could have given you more, I am telling you that they gave you the biggest gift one can ever receive. We all receive it and it is enough for all of us to succeed in this life. This gift, is the gift of life itself. A life that most people take for granted daily. Your parents brought you here on this earth regardless if you were planned or not, if you were wanted or not. The fact that you are still here proves that you have what it takes to make your dreams happen at this very moment.

Regardless of the challenges you will have to face, you have faced the biggest one yet. You made it through the process of being born. You are here now despite the miniscule odd of your survival through your mother's womb. You made it. You are alive and that should be enough for you to keep pushing forward until you get what you want to have in life. Some people blame their peers but I'm telling you that you can't put that blame on them. Your peers are on the same road that you are on therefore you need to be faster than them and more effective. Ensure that you will work hard towards your happiness. If you cannot beat them then work harder until you do. Stop blaming them for they are putting in the time and the energy necessary to make their dreams a reality. They are giving it all they have to ensure that they get there. The question is are YOU giving it <u>your</u> all?

I need you to give it all you have and push until your dream becomes a reality as well. The only person you can blame here if you do not succeed is yourself. For only you have the power to push yourself beyond your limits. Do not forget that your "why" will help and your values will bring the support that you need as well. There is a quote from Albert Einstein that I love and that I have used as a key concept in my personal journey. I briefly mentioned this earlier but I still need you to keep it in your mind and I will keep bringing it up until the time comes for me to go in greater details in its explanation. He says: "Try not to become a man of success but a man of value". Here, he does not use the word success in a monetary setting. In other words, try as much as possible not to run after money. I briefly touched up on this earlier and asked you to run towards your self-defined success by avoiding to think about the money you could make from that dream you were given.

In the following chapters, I will go into greater details in the understanding that success should never relate to only money. In other words, you are not successful because you are rich. As stated before, money comes and goes, whereas success stays throughout history. Once you understand the difference between success and money, the next step will call on you to take a leap forward to focus on achieving that goal that you want to accomplish. Remember that the only person who can do it in YOUR life is you therefore start working now and see the fruits of your hard labor flourish.

This step is one of the longest yet the most important and the hardest one to work on. What I have realised throughout my life and my personal experience is that your values are closely connected with your emotions. This means that if you are guided by good values, the emotions that will be attached to said values usually are good. This is why it is important to be in touch with your emotions for they will guide you on your path. Listen to your emotions and follow your heart for only there lies your true feelings and desires. At this very moment, you are called to work on your emotions in great detail so as to get to the point of true happiness. This happiness will quickly become one of your most precious assets. An asset, I truly hope that you will cherish all your life. Use it to your advantage when going through the hard and the good times because only good things can come out of it.

CHAPTER 9

GENERAL EMOTIONS

When we talk about emotions, I need you to understand that emotions are almost never logical. Rarely can you truly explain the way you feel and the person that is listening will feel the same emotions. This is because emotions reside in the realm of the illogical because you feel your own emotions and everybody else feels their own emotions.

Let me take a moment to illustrate the importance of your emotions. Everything that happens to you in this life will affect you emotionally. You are thus governed by your emotions. Your emotions are one of the best way for you to figure out what your point of view is in regards to a specific situation. Think about it, when you are sad, you want the pain to stop therefore you try and run away from your pains or any situations that hurt you without taking the time to fully understand the reason why you got hurt. When you are mad, you usually make bad decisions in regards to the situation that you are facing because your anger clouds your mind and you are not capable of thinking "rationally" [9] in those situations.

When you are happy, you think of other happy moments and you have an amazing day. You thus run after happiness over and over again without fully grasping the notion of happiness nor the key points in the situation that make you happy. You only chronically chase or replicate the situation in the hopes that happiness will once again be present. Hopefully you get where I am getting with this. Your emotions are a part of you and therefore you need to learn to control them while they guide you.

---

[9]   Rationally: Here the brackets express the subjective nature of rationality. We define what reason is and what it is not, therefore what is rational depends on our subjective point of view.

An amazing saying that I wake up to every single morning is that: "Life is not measured by the number of breaths you take but by the moments that take your breath away" (Vicki Corona). It is important to me that you make sure that the moments that take your breath away are worth it. The trap with this is that regardless if you are angry, sad or happy, most of the time you will lose your breath for a short period of time. This mechanism is available to us so we can be aware of the moments that affect us emotionally. We are in touch with our emotions regardless of the nature of our emotion (sad, angry, happy, disappointed, etc.). We will succumb to them and follow the path that they put down for us. If we do not learn to listen to them with a great deal of wisdom and control them to ensure that we are guided by them, we will get dragged by them down a path that we can categorise as massively destructive.

Don't forget that if you can control your emotions, you will be able to adjust and align yourself with great values that will push you towards blazing your personal trail. It is important that you understand that, till this point, I have made a brief allusion to only three emotions. This is mostly due to the fact that those three emotions are, to my theory and belief, the three primary governing emotions. You bear a great number of emotions that are confined within the limits of a spectre. I always laugh when I present this theory in this particular way because it is a funny way of portraying the illusionistic aspect of your emotions. To fully grasp this theory, you first need to understand that a spectre has no limits which basically means that by "logical deduction"[10], your emotions are limitless. In the realm of this book, I will focus on a very small portion of your emotions. We will only focus on single emotions here and not stray to the interesting complexity of mixed emotions. With that being said, we will focus only on 6 main emotions.

1. Fear
2. Anger
3. Sadness

4. Shame
5. Pain
6. Happiness

We will go through each of those 6 emotions individually and uncover their power along the way. Like stated before, try to tap into your emotions and use them to your advantage for they are here to guide you. You might as well try your best to be guided by positive emotions to ensure a great deal of positive results.

---

[10] Logical Deduction: We try to find logic in the surreal realm of this spectre that will define a logic train of ideas that will reach a define goal that matches the first premise that was evoked. Thus, the first conclusion made will be the same as the final conclusion when operating in a deductive reasoning scenario.

CHAPTER 10

SPECIFIC EMOTIONS

FEAR

The first emotion that you need to be aware of is fear. As you know and experience it all the time, everybody is afraid of something. It could be from the smallest ant to the wind that blows or the lion that roars. I have friends that are afraid of birds or worms. Regardless of what you are afraid of, one thing is universal and certain, everybody feels fear at some point in their lives. You need to know that FEAR is only what you make it. This basically means that you subconsciously create your fears. Don't get me wrong, there are some things that are worth being afraid of. Fear helps us survive dangerous situations. If a lion is ready to pounce on you, your fear is what makes you react to the situation. Pay close attention to what I just said. Your FEAR makes you REACT. This means that certain people have a sudden burst of energy when they are afraid in specific situations. Unfortunately, some people react differently than others. If you take the same situation stated above, some people will freeze and won't be able to do anything in that situation.

Let's examine both outcomes for a moment. In certain situations, it is good that fear gives you energy and helps you run very fast or jump tall walls. In other situations, it is best to stay still and not move. To survive those situations, it is to your advantage when you freeze. But in both cases, your fear brings you energy. The difference lies in the way that energy is used. In the first one, the energy is released externally and you activate your muscles with that said energy. In the second outcome, you use that energy to inhibit your muscles (unconsciously). It is important to know that it takes a great deal of energy to inhibit your muscles. Therefore we can honestly say that you will get a great deal of energy from your fear most of the time.

I always like to think of fear as an equivalent to darkness. You don't know what will happen when you are afraid, you don't know how you will react and when you are afraid you rarely think of what is going on at the moment. You just act in the heart of the action. Therefore you are in complete darkness not knowing what's going on, what will happen, where you are. Since you don't know, the only thing left for you to do is act. This is one of the reasons that people are afraid of the dark. Since people don't know much about the darkness and since they can't even see in the dark, they cannot predict what is coming towards them nor how they will react.

Let me put you in a specific context that I got from Eric Thomas: in the Batman movie, Bane said something that caught my attention. We all know that Batman mastered the art of being the dark knight, he trained hard in the dark and therefore he has an advantage in the dark because he learned to use it in his favor. When he goes against Bane and starts losing, he started turning off all the lights because in his mind, he is Batman and he has an advantage in the dark. Bane laughs and says: "You trained in the dark, you adapted to the dark. I was **BORN** in the dark, **SHAPED** by the dark, **MOLDED** by the dark." Bane who was born in the dark, knows nothing else but the dark. If you know nothing else but the unpredictable, then what else can you be afraid of? He learned to use the power of darkness since he had no other choice of powers and environment to deal with. He had to live with whatever was going to happen. Regardless of what would come in front of him or behind him, he had to be ready for it and take it head on into battle. By doing this, you will achieve victory.

Victory gives us energy that we can use to keep pushing forward but, victory can be a very dangerous asset to have in your arsenal if used the wrong way and at the wrong time. Let's go back to the Batman scenario and extract more knowledge. Batman has won a lot of battles, therefore he is accustom to victory. It is a good thing because that gives him hope and faith that he will keep on winning. The danger of victory comes in a very simple yet unique phrase that Bane points out. Batman starts pushing Bane and throws many punches that usually do the job against other criminals that he had to face. Bane just looks at him unfazed and unhurt from those punches and says : "victory has defeated you". This phrase is very powerful because, at first glance, we think that it contradicts itself. Upon great reflection and meditation upon said phrase, it makes great sense and unloads great wisdom upon us. You are so accustom to winning that you have become conceded in your victory. You are used to winning therefore you think that you will always win so you don't put in the necessary energy to keep pushing towards your victory. So again "victory has defeated you". You need to know that it is good to win but you must always be afraid of losing and by being afraid of losing you are forcing yourself to always push towards victory by using fear and not take for granted that you will always win. This fear will bring you the necessary power that you need. It is now up to you to use that power effectively and rejoice in the amazing results that will come to past.

With great power comes great responsibility. You need to learn how to control that power. If you can control your emotions, you can control the power that they bring you and make sure that you use that power towards a specific goal to remedy the situation that you are facing. In regards to fear, you need to know that they are not real. You create them therefore you have the power to destroy them when you want to.

I came across an acronym once that affirmed a great mental offset to live by : "False Evidence Appearing Real (FEAR)" (author unknown). There is no real evidence for fear. If there were, than we would not be able to get over our fears and everybody would be afraid of the same thing. Since we create our fears, with the right tools we can also disarm them and then put them away. Think of all the people that achieved success. They did so by being afraid of failing. Since they possessed the desire to kill that fear, the only way of literally disarming that fear was by making sure that they succeeded. It is an undeniable truth that you will be afraid but if you get passed those fears, run towards your problems with guns blazing and just start shooting them down one by one, you will see great progress. On the flip side, they are just as well trying to shoot you down and unfortunately (fortunately as well as you will discover) some of them might land a bullet in you that will knock you down and put you in the hospital. This is when you will need to greatly think about, recuperate, reload and go get your revenge by going against that obstacle and showing it that you are now stronger, faster and smarter because of it and this time you take it down once and for all.

Use your fears to power your hunger towards success because when you are hungry, you will try your best to find food and satisfy said hunger. You need to be hungry for your personal success and it is your duty to fear not having the possibility to eat. Only then will you be able to force yourself to kill that fear by achieving success and finally savouring your hard earned success. Walter Scott said that: "The rose is fairest when it is budding new, and hope is brightest when it downs from fears". Therefore you need to use that fear to hope for massive success in accomplishing your dreams and finally turning them into reality. Hope not for a better life but hope for the energy to go against your trials and tribulations while coming out victorious from the battle field. You are the champion of your life and you can achieve greatness only if you work hard and knock down every problems that is put in front of you.

ANGER

The second emotion that you need to work on is anger. Emotions usually happen without your consent which means that you cannot stop them but you can control specific aspects of your environment that have certain effects on your emotions. A situation will present itself that will affect you negatively if you do not take care of it on the spot. You need to know that anger is like a curse. You can't easily break a curse but you can turn it to your advantage. If you take in and understand the notion that you can live with a curse without letting that curse consume you, that curse will become a part of you. You can use it to your advantage just like the previous emotion that we worked on.

Anger greatly deteriorates your hard work. If you do not take care of that curse, it will kill all the hard work that you have been putting into play. If it does not kill it, it will diminish and belittle its value. By letting your anger kill your work, you will have to redo all the work that you did to get back to where you were before your anger consumed you. The negative aspect of a curse is that if you do not lift it, it will reoccur over and over again until it is duly dealt with. If you deal with it, gradually, you will strengthen your values because anger, like stated before, acts like a poison that will destroy your values. If you do not have good values, you will not be able to achieve your dreams therefore you need to control your emotions thus control your anger to ensure that your values stay intact. Since anger is not beneficial, it is up to you to use the same theory as before.

When you get mad, instead of letting that anger consume you and fall in the trap of ruining your goals, just try and use that energy by translating it into time and effort you desperately need in order to achieve your goals. When you are mad, instead of cursing out everybody and the situation, you need to remember that everybody goes through hard times and once you can take that in, you will need to use the rising energy and put it towards finding a solutions instead of just throwing a tantrum because that tantrum will not fix the problem. You will use up the energy that you have just acquired by throwing a tantrum which is a good thing to a certain extent. But at the end of that tantrum, you will not have accomplished anything useful. Therefore, being angry never solves any of the problems that you are facing. The only thing that you will accomplish by being angry is waste useful energy in meaningless actions. Being angry usually worsens the situation and will create new problems that will also have to be dealt with in due time. Anger will bring about more problems, which in return will cause more distress which can once again lead to possible added anger. This creates an uncomfortable and useless cycle. Anger creates problems that bring about distress which calls back more anger and so on. Can one truly live happily in this situation?

Think of it this way: When you are angry, you act like a volcano that builds up all the magma but doesn't let it out. Energy builds up in that volcano over time and eventually that volcano erupts. It erupts and releases that energy violently and causes a great deal of destruction everywhere that magma/energy will reach. Surprisingly enough, as powerful as that volcano is, once the magma reaches water, it calms down and loses all its energy along the way. More and more magma will reach the water but the water keeps on cooling the magma down by taking away its energy.

Here is what is spectacular about this phenomena, the water evaporates when it comes in contact with the magma. The magma solidifies and will not move beyond that point because the water takes the energy away from it. That evaporated water builds up in the sky and uses that energy to pour back down in the ocean. Therefore, the ocean never really loses anything since the water always comes back over and over again regardless of what happens. When rain falls, the surrounding plants get watered and they can bloom with rich spectacular colors which represent the second positive outcome of the initially tragic event. You need to act like water and use the energy of your anger to add to your hard work so you can grow more and flourish. Eventually, that hard work will pay off and just like the ocean gets back its water, you will rejoice with the fruits of your actions and hard work. Only then will you know and understand the importance of using negative aspects of your life to your advantage. You are in control so you might as well steer in the direction that you want to reach your final objective.

SADNESS

The third emotion that you need to work on is your sadness. Contrary to common belief, sadness is a very good thing to experience. By being sad, you allow yourself to tap into your deep rooted emotions which in return will open the door to other emotions that are more complex and more beneficial for you. These complex emotions will bring you to a whole new level in your life and you will see great new positive outcomes in front of you.

We tend to block out anything that can hurt us. We are afraid of rejection and personal injuries to a point that we will just avoid any situation that affects us negatively. If there is one thing that I learned throughout my journey, it is that if you go through true profound sadness, you will feel very demoralized and drained. The silver lining to this dark cloud is that it will open the door to greater and more positive emotions that will fill your heart up only if you allow them to do so. Most people feel lonely and sad on a regular basis and unfortunately try block out that sadness with temporary, meaningless actions that they think bring them happiness. When most people are alone, they run to their phones and try to contact other people for reassurance and comfort. Unfortunately, that kind of happiness is very temporary and therefore it will not bring great value to your life. The only outcome to this will be sadness each and every single time you end up alone.

It is important, for your own sake, to stand strong during the sad times by letting it affect you and get through it. By doing so, you make sure for one, that you will be able to go through that situation at any given moment in the future. Since you now know how to deal with it, you will achieve a certain level of serenity that will be hard to break because it is deeply rooted in your inner being. You will become a stronger, better individual if you go through those hard, challenging times. Ponder on this for one second, since sadness promotes growth and improvement, you can easily use that personal growth to open the doors to the other emotions that are hidden within your heart.

This being said, you will hopefully realize that once you push through, the biggest reward for you in this turmoil phase will be that the door to your heart and your love will open. Only then will you be able to completely share your love with those that you choose to give it to and that deserve it. The positive side to this is that if ever anyone does <u>TRY</u> and break your heart, since you have learned to go through pain and sadness, you will "easily" get back on your feet regardless of how deeply you were hurt. It might take more time to get back from it, but eventually you will since you have the knowledge to overcome pain. You will believe that you are capable of overcoming it thus you will act upon that personal belief of yours. You should never let sadness govern your life. Always learn from your sadness and pain until you reach profound serenity which will eventually bring you joy, happiness and love for not only yourself, but also for everything and everyone else that you wish to share said love with over and over again.

You will go through a cycle of never ending joy and love that you will want to share with the world and you will receive love and joy from most people in your life as part of that cycle. This gift that you will receive will thus make you want to give even more peace, love and joy to more people and thus restart the process over and over again.

SHAME

Shame will either be your biggest ally or the tool of your demise. If there is one thing that I can assure you of, it is that you have at some point in your life experienced shame. You have to work on this emotion in order to progress in life and develop yourself completely. The feeling of shame can build very powerful self-destructive energy in your mind that will slowly destroy you. Most people are ashamed of following their dreams because they do not want to be seen as a failure. They are ashamed of the words that other people use when they refer to them and how their decisions will affect their lives.

Unfortunately, most people with these types of thinking processes, fail miserably in life. The biggest reason for said failure is their fear of others saying that they are failures. Sadly, this becomes a self-fulfilling prophecy in the sense that they do not act on their dreams because they do not want to be ashamed by their failures and be perceived as unsuccessful people. The self-fulfilling prophecy occurs when they don't act on their dreams and ideas, they automatically become failures. They have not acted on their personal dreams and therefore automatically fail to make those dreams become reality. It starts to decay and rot in their thoughts and that will affect their actions and pollute their dreams.

You need to remember that it is your life and you should <u>NEVER</u> be afraid of going after your goals. Shame should never be a part of your life because if you are ashamed of failing and you don't take action, you automatically FAIL and you will be miserable until you change your perception of failure. As a result of said failure, you do not work on your dreams and you won't be happy at any given point in your life unless you make the CONSCIOUS decision to start working on making those dreams become a reality. Ponder carefully on the following phrase: if you are not happy, what is your life truly worth and do you believe that you would be able to live in an unfulfilled life while you are intentionally dodging your personal goals with your lack of action? Don't they deserve to be honored because they belong to you and only you? Don't you deserve to be happy?

The logical answer to those questions resides in the actions and decisions that you took thus far. If you chose to ignore the ideas and dreams that came to you, I can guarantee you that you will be miserable in your life and you will always ask yourself the ironic and redundant question : <u>WHAT IF I</u> actually did it and it worked? Since you will not be able to answer that question, it will haunt you for the rest of your life. Imagine living a life asking yourself a question that you can never answer. What kind of a life is that truly? Can you see yourself living a haunting life with unanswered questions? The only way to avoid this situation is to actually put in the time, the energy and complete passion working on those dreams. Remember to put aside any shame that you have and just take action. You will experience the results that will come regardless of the path that you have chosen. Why not ensure that the results are enjoyable for you? You should believe that you deserve it and work towards that goal.

PAIN

I cannot stress on how this particular feeling is hated and avoided in our society. In the time and days that we live in, most people will try as much as possible to avoid any situation that will bring them pain. It is quite obvious that inflicting self-pain is a serious matter that needs to be dealt with accordingly. In a scenario where a situation, out of direct control, tends to bring pain to an individual, the most common reaction is to run away from that situation and distance oneself from the pain as much as possible.

Pain can be an ally if you learn to deal with it accordingly. A common misconception about pain is that it lasts forever and your suffering will increase exponentially throughout time. If you are used to thinking in this way, I need you to let go of that mentality at this very moment. You need to understand that pain is temporary. If you truly think about it, are you hurting right now? To those who unfortunately answered yes, think of a previous pain that you have had to go through. Now think of the time lap between the previous and the present pain that you are going through. Even if it is one day, this proves that eventually, your pain will subside. You might experience painful situations again. Nonetheless, you will have a certain amount of time in between both situations during which, you will not feel any pain. The pain that you are feeling at this very moment may last a week, maybe a month, maybe a year or even maybe just a couple of minutes in regards to minor pains but eventually, that pain will disappear and you will go back to being "normal"[11]. You need to be aware of the fact that pain will be present but only for a set amount of time that can never be pre-determined.

On another note, since pain will be present either way, you need to know that if you go through pain, you will become stronger than you were before. The positive attribute of pain is that it is usually followed by wisdom and knowledge. Once you get hurt, you automatically learn that you did not like that situation and now you know how to avoid it. Let me be clear, that knowledge will not come to you if you do not go through the initial pain. Since most people run from their pain and don't face it, they do not get the opportunity to learn and evolve from that situation. They will be faced with that same situation and will not know how to deal with it. You need to remember that knowledge contains power and an individual who possesses specific power becomes more and more powerful through pain and suffering.

---

[11]   Normal: Normality is greatly subjective. Remember that you define what is normal to you. As much as it might be abnormal to someone else it does not mean that it is wrong. Charles Adams once said "Normal is an illusion. What is normal for the spider is chaos for the fly".

Here is the small but manageable dark side of having power. Remember that with great power comes great responsibility. You need to grow emotionally and develop your inner wisdom to use your knowledge towards good deeds and actions. This will help you prepare a better future for yourself, a future where with your knowledge, your wisdom and your ability to withstand pain, you will eventually make your dreams come true and achieve happiness. Let the pain hit you like it was a rock that was thrown at you. It will hurt, you will suffer but the knowledge that you will gain from it will be priceless because now you will have learned to dodge the painful punch that life enjoys throwing at us on a regular basis. If that initial rock didn't hit you, you would have never learned this important life lesson. It is due to the pain that you felt that you now know to move and avoid being hit. Pain has given you the possibility to remember that suffering and quickly dodge that projectile and show you that you are faster now than you were before.

The next step from there will be for you to duly apply that knowledge to your life over and over again and gain experience along the way. Eventually the pain will go away and will be replaced with success and happiness while you make sure that the knowledge is used in the event that the situation shows up again and now you can avoid that pain and maybe eventually fight back if necessary. You will learn to go beyond pain and achieve a level of relief that will help you get pass specific hurtful situations. Learn to forgive and learn to move forward for what happened in the past will always be in the past. Never dwell on a past experience and let it have a negative impact on your present life. Behind great pain there is always also great happiness. The only thing you have to do is go through that pain, endure it until it doesn't hurt anymore and it dies out for then and only then can you experience extraordinary happiness.

HAPPINESS

I know that you probably were asking yourself why I focused so much on negative emotions knowing that there are so many other emotions that are so positive in life. It is simply because, regardless of the numerous negative emotions that you feel, if you have just one positive emotion really fill your heart, the negative ones automatically lose all their power and control that they had over you. Like stated before, once you go through certain negative emotions, you will eventually feel a certain level of happiness that you cannot find without the previous work. The work that needs to be done here is to challenge your negative emotions, fight them and true profound happiness will make its way to you. If you do not face them, you will forever live in negativity and where there is negativity, happiness is rarely present.

A very special quote given to us by Aristotle states that "Happiness is the highest good, being a realization and perfect practice of virtue, which some can attain, while others have little or none of it [...]". It is certain that everyone wants to be happy but unfortunately most people aren't. The reason for that is because they do not walk the hidden path [12] to happiness. Most people are content with the life that they currently have but if you ask them what would make them happy, everyone will give you a specific thing that they would like to have or achieve that will bring them happiness. In that case, you are not really happy until you get what you want. You might be content but not truly happy. You will finally witness the discrepancy in the realm of personal happiness when you achieve your desired goal. We do not all want the same things in life therefore what will bring me happiness might not bring it to you. Fight for what YOU want.

Unfortunately, most people will not put in the necessary energy to uncover the hidden path towards their happiness and prefer staying in contentment. There is a powerful quote that I came across one day while walking down the streets. "Why is it that people prefer known hell as opposed to unknown heaven?" (Author unknown). This quote perfectly illustrates the point that I made earlier. Most people are content with their lives, therefore they prefer staying in their known hell and avoid exploring the unknown heavens that are within their reach. That should bring up so many questions to each and every one of you but unfortunately, nobody can give you the answer to those questions.

Only you know the path to follow to achieve the coveted enlightenment and reach your personal happiness. I am only here to push you forward and get you to start walking in the necessary direction. Sidney J. Harris once said "Happiness is a direction, not a place". So believe in yourself and start traveling in the direction of your happiness which will come to you gradually with each step that you will take. I love the previous quote because it goes hand in hand with a quote from Jim Rohn which implies that "Happiness doesn't come from big pieces of great success but from small, daily achievements hammered down day by day with as much **precision** as possible". If you want to build a house, you need to make sure to have the plans drawn for that house. Once the plans are made, you work on the foundation of the house. Once the foundation is laid, you will need to make sure that each and every stone or brick that is laid down is done with the upmost perfection. Day by day, you lay brick after

---

[12] Hidden path: I want to make sure you get the notion of hidden path here. There is not a set path for you to follow to be happy. Like I have said on numerous occasion throughout this book, you create your own path with the different decisions that you will have to take. Therefore your path is and will remain hidden and only you can discover it step by step.

brick with precision and eventually you will have a strong, stable structure that will be able to withstand anything. If there is something that eventually breaks it down and trust me, there will be, you will learn from your mistakes. These lessons learned will help you rebuild that structure while respecting the new specifications required for it to withstand the threat that initially brought it down. This will prevent the reoccurrence of that destructive situation. Learn from your mistakes and from your past.

Be grateful for what you have at every moment of your life because since the day you were born you were given the most precious gifts in the world. The gift of life, the gift of knowledge and the gift of emotions. With all of these working together, you can do anything you want to do by adapting to multiple situations that will come towards you. You already have them in you so why not start using them as we speak in order to get you to your happiness as soon as possible.

CHAPTER 11

OPINION

Your opinion of yourself is going to be the biggest shock that you ever had in your life. We tend to be extremely critical and harsh with ourselves. It is important that you take the time to develop and question your self-opinion. The reason for this lies in the domain of self-concept. You need to understand that your self-concept and self-perception are very strong assets to possess in a process as long and difficult as achieving your dream. Most people put so much energy into the image that other people have of them that they lose the importance of self-oppinion. When you start putting energy on what other people are thinking, you will only focus on fixing what they think is a problem. The trap here is that you are working on making them happy regardless if you will be happy or not. The point of following your dream is for you to achieve happiness and not work to implicitly make someone else's happiness come true.

You need to know that regardless of what other people tell you, you need to do what you want to do while making sure that you do not hurt anyone in the process. I learned a very important ideology through the teachings of Les Brown which he himself learned at a young age from Mr. Leroy Washington which basically says that "someone's opinion of you does not have to become your reality". What Mr. Washington tried to teach Mr. Brown was to not let someone define who you are. You have control over your life as I mentioned previously. If this is truly the case, then what good can it bring you to let someone change your personality or your way of being? You will never truly be happy if you are not being yourself and you are only working on making other people's visions come true. Remember that these people might not necessarily care about your personal feelings and dreams for they only want to get ahead in life until they achieve their personal goals. Those who want to see you happy and who truly care about you will try their best to support your ideas and will try to help you through your struggles.

Ralph Waldo Emerson once said that "most of the shadows of this life are caused by our own standing in our own sunshine". The easiest way to explain this is by giving you an example. Let's say somebody told you that what you were doing was wrong and for some inexplicable reason, you decided to believe him. The reason why he was capable of affecting your emotions and values, is because you gave him that power. The results of this particular situation is represented by your shadow and your shadow only appears when you are present. The sun sends down its rays on you and the result of the rays hitting your body will be a shadow because your body was there to block those rays while they try to affect you. By analogy, if someone throws their opinion or point of view towards you, your body and your mind will interact with those point of views. The difference lies in the extensive variations of your shadow. It is interesting to experience the following : if you change positions, the shadow that you were casting before will change form. You control the appearance of the shadow by changing positions. For example, by changing from a frontal stance towards a profile stance, you undeniably will get a different shadow. Try lifting your hands up or down, try putting your hands together. What you need to understand is that you control the shadow that will result from the light hitting your body, just like you can control the way you react to what other people will say. The analogy here is to show you that when people give you their opinion on a situation that affects you personally, YOU and only you have control on the resulting shadow. Your reaction and self-concept of that person's opinion will determine the result of this particular conversation.

If you possess a strong self-concept, you will be able to shape your result because you decide how those rays are going to hit you and thus you will be able to create the shadow that you want. "One way to get the most out of life is to look upon it as an adventure" (William Feather). Have fun in creating different new shadows until you find the one that suits you regardless of what other people say. Since your shadow is a reflection of yourself, then you need to make sure that you create a shadow that will keep you happy and excited on a regular basis. "To be happy, we must not be concerned with others", (Albert Camus), because "happiness depends upon ourselves" (Aristotle). When you are capable of grasping the notion of those two quotes completely, you will be capable of reaching a portion of your personal happiness and add it to what you have already accomplished along the way. I told you before that "happiness does not come from big pieces of great success, but from small advantages hammered down day by day", (Jim Rohn). You need to work on perfecting your shadow by working on your personal opinion every single day and eventually, you will be able to automatically define your own reality in most situations that will present themselves to you.

People will always have an opinion about your life and about your choices but never forget that both your life and your choices belong to you and only you, which means that you are the only one that should have any control or effect on them. We will end this chapter with a quote from Sir. J. Stephen that says : "Every man has in himself a continent of undiscovered character. Happy is he who acts as the Columbus to his own soul". Be your own navigator and drive yourself towards your personal goal. Do not worry about the opinion of others as long as you figure out what you truly want and what makes you happy. Keep pushing towards perfecting yourself day by day. Once you have mastered this concept of self-opinion, you will be mentally ready to receive the amazing theory that is presented in the next chapter. You truly will need to concentrate on understanding this theory because it lies in the domain of the surreal. This implies that you will have to truly think about manifesting this theory and implement it in your daily activities.

CHAPTER 12

I AM THAT, I AM

If you followed and understood the previous chapter accordingly, you are now ready to receive this new critical information. If you truly understand this theory, you will achieve a new level of wisdom that you probably never achieved so far in your life. This theory came to me through research that was made by Rhonda Byrne in one of her books. You are at this very moment entering the realm of "I AM THAT, I AM". It is primordial for the advancement of your dream and project that you understand this. It is a way for you to understand the path that you are gradually creating and thus discovering.

The best way to understand this concept of "I AM THAT, I AM," is to go to the roots where it was created. "I AM THAT, I AM" is God's name. This name represents the biggest secret and power that we can ever have. When God came to Moses, he presented himself to Moses by saying "I am that I am". In the Christian New Testament, God is quoted as saying "I am the Alpha and the Omega, the First and the Last, the Beginning and the End". In other words, God is, has and always will be everything. He is the first, and will be the last without any doubt. I want to be clear that I am not preaching a religious point of view here. I am talking about a higher form that is as well represented in science by the smallest atom that constitutes the smallest entity of every object or living creature on this planet. There is a scientific theory that explains the eventuality to become whatever we would want to if we could manipulate our atoms the way we desired. For the sake of the illustration, I will keep with the explanation used by Mrs. Byrne.

With this explained, I want to bring us back to the original wording that I presented to you "I AM THAT, I AM". I want to focus your attention on the most important part of that phrase and yet the smallest part of it. The most important part of that phrase is surprisingly the coma. The coma in that phrase is the only way for the said phrase to actually make any sense. God is saying that he is "THAT" ("THAT" basically represents anything you want in the world). He then puts the coma there to mark a pause which reinforces reflection upon the previous statement. Afterwards, he emphasizes again on the belief that HE IS THAT, with great confidence. This is how I came to understand it : God is for example, the tree or the wind that blows or the ocean and the waves or any creature on this planet but never forget that he is "THAT", which is why the second part of the name is so important. God told us that we were created in his image and by analogy, since God is all, we also are all. We are connected to everything. Science has just as well proved that we are all made of the same matter and therefore we are all everything and everything is us as well.

Here is where the previous chapter comes into play. If you have developed a strong self-opinion, you will need to understand that you are who you say you are. It should never matter what other people think of you. What truly matters, is that you know deep inside who you truly are and you work on following that personal path. You do not judge a tree by the fruits that it talks about. You judge a tree by the fruit that it bears. People will not judge you with the words that you say. On the contrary, they will judge you by your actions and the results that you produce. Always remember that since you were created in God's image, you too have the power to be and do anything you want so it is about time you work hard at it in order to accomplish it. While I was doing some research on this theory, I discovered an amazing message that explains in great detail the unique name of GOD.

<u>G</u>iving
<u>O</u>neness
<u>D</u>estiny

GIVING

This acronym is extremely important to understand the currently used wording of his name. The "G" stands for giving because God is a giving entity. Regardless the religion we follow, the God that is praised has always been an unconditionally giving lord in many domains. He possesses so much love for us that he rarely will deny us anything. He listens to our prayers and always provides us with the resources to fulfill our needs. Be careful in distinctly separating needing something and wanting something. There is a small saying that always gives me hope during my hard times which is expressed the following way: "Life never gives you something that he knows you cannot handle". If you are going through a rough time right now, you can be assured that life knows that you have the power to overcome it and better yourself if you dedicate yourself enough in solving the problem. Life is giving you a difficult situation in the hopes that you will accept the challenge and push forward until you fix the problem and become a better person in the process. Life is hard for a reason. If you did not earn something, you cannot maintain it. When you go through hard situations, you push yourself to your limits and earn the spot that you will reach. Sadly, when you stay stuck in a negative spot, it is unfortunately what you have earned by not giving your all to reach the goal. Wherever you are in life, you deserve to be there because you are listening to the barriers that are inside of you, the barriers that are stopping you from getting the abundant life that you want to have.

ONENESS

The "O" stands for Oneness which refers directly to the idea that we are all connected to everything one way or another. Remember that we are created in the image of God and God is everything. Thus, one will argue that we are everything as well. Bear with me here because unfortunately and fortunately, it is a bit more complicated than it seems. You need to understand that we are not only the reflection of God but we are one with God and every living and non-living thing on this earth. We are spiritually (to the atomic level) connected to every organism on this planet regardless if said organism be a living organism or not. This implies that we are connected to anything and everything at all times during and even after our lives.

We learn at a very young age to disassociate ourselves from the rest of the world and only to focus on our eyesight. In other words, we focus on what our eyes are showing us. I need you to start using your insight because your insight focuses on your ways of seeing the world and not on what stimuli your eyes are receiving. If you can learn to go beyond what you see and input what you feel into the equation, you will awaken your insight and realize that everything is connected (to each other). In the book Le Petit Prince, Antoine de Saint-Exupéry explains that "the essential things in life are usually invisible to the eyes". How do you know that what you see with your eyes is the truth? Question what you see because most of the time if you blindfold yourself, you will experience something greater than what you are used to seeing. Scientists define this concept as a unified field. We are all a part of a field that bonds us to each other physically, mentally and spiritually. If we can tap into this lifestyle, we will be in tune with the world and everything surrounding us will work with us towards our happiness.

You will be able to work faster and with greater ease since you will be getting help from wherever it is needed and available.

The beauty of this concept is that you will worry less about the negativity that exists in the world because you have finally realised that the negativity is also a part of the unified field. The negativity that we greatly frown upon in our society brings glorious gifts that we tend to ignore. To truly be in tune with the world, you need to acknowledge the negativity that you possess and then you will be able to see and use the gifts that accompany it. By analysing the darkness that surrounds you, you will be able to find the light that the darkness has been hiding for so long. You will treasure that light even more. The reason for this is because said light was so important that the darkness wanted to keep it for itself. Just remember that when you go treasure hunting, the treasure is always hidden in the most unconventional and hard to reach places but once you make it there, you will understand that the journey is just as important, if not more so, than the treasures found. The journey, by itself, brings knowledge and wisdom that are amazing assets to have and should already be considered invaluable. When you add that knowledge to the treasure that you have discovered, there is not much that can stop you from moving forward. You will then rejoice in the oneness that you are a part of and you will learn from every single experience you will go through to be able to strengthen your bond with everything.

DESTINY

This brings us to the last letter in God's name which is the "D". It is connected to the Oneness of the world because, thanks to that concept, you will be able to follow your destiny. I truly believe that we create our own destiny. But we create it by taking decisions in our lives and acting out on these decisions. I believe that when one is connected to his environment, then he is capable of making informed decisions that will positively affect his life. Do not forget that even when you make a bad decision, there is a silver lining which you can lean on and learn from your mistakes. This clearly shows that your destiny is in your hands because your decisions will reveal the following stepping stone of your personal path. Each step you take is a decision you take which will in turn reveal a new stone and so on thus, once again, showing the relevance and importance of the concept of oneness.

You need to be aware of what your calling is and I truly believe that we define our calling. Some people want to bring medical support to this world, others want to bring marvellous musical art to this world. Since we are all different, we will have different callings. I personally want to bring motivational support to each and every one of my readers in the hopes that they start working towards their calling. I need you to get in touch with your destiny and just envision your life as a whole and just imagine what the journey that you must take is going to be in order to achieve your personal happiness. Once you find that and you start believing that you are worth experiencing that true happiness, then you will need to start taking decisions to better your life and follow your personal destiny.

Only when you combine all of these concepts and truly implement them to your life, will you be able to understand that your life is worth living with complete joy and happiness towards everything and everyone. There is a saying that I came across during my research on the concept of "I AM THAT, I AM" which brings one to truly think and evaluate life continuously. "The understanding about THAT, and the living from THAT is the journey". This means that you need to understand and grasp the concept that you are "THAT" (whatever you want to be) and if you truly live your life with that mentality, your journey will be filled with joy, happiness and personal achievements since your life will have been based on what you truly wanted it to be based on. You will feel complete and you will want to share your newly discovered gifts with the world, the ONE WORLD that you are learning to be one with.

CHAPTER 13

HARD WORK

I know that I have been mentioning this throughout the whole book but I feel that it is too important to not have its own chapter. There is no way I could illustrate how much hard work you need to put in to get what you really want. Like I said before, most people want fame, glory, success, happiness or anything that a person can want out of life but unfortunately, they do not put in any effort in order to achieve that goal. Some people want to become models, or actors but they do not practice those arts a single day of their lives. They expect it to just happen from one day to the next.

Here is the cruel truth, most successful people that made their dreams become a reality know that they got what they now have because they were willing to put in the necessary work. I am here to tell you right now that you must be willing to do what most people won't do. If you want to become a successful business man, then you need to start investing time, effort and money into your project. You might need to take some classes to improve your management skills, read some books on how to manage your business but one thing is certain, you will need to take the time to put in the effort in getting the necessary knowledge that is needed for the goal that you want to achieve. If you truly want to become stronger, you don't stay in bed every single day. Instead you wake up earlier every morning and you work out and force your muscles to grow bigger and stronger every single day. I was researching for a motivational session when I came across a quote from T. E. Lawrence that is extremely powerful if you take the time to truly analyse it meticulously. The quote states that:

"All men dream, but not equally. Those who dream by night in the dusty recesses of their minds, wake in the day to find that it was vanity: but the dreamers of the day are dangerous men, for they may act on their dreams with open eyes, to make them possible"

He brings a new concept to the table that I have been trying to teach you since the beginning of this book. He says that it is important to differentiate dreaming while sleeping from dreaming while being awake. I truly believe in what T. E. Lawrence says. Most people who dream while they are sleeping will most likely never be successful in their lives. When you are sleeping and you dream, first of all, there is a great chance that you will forget that dream. Second of all, you cannot control those dreams since they lie in the realm of the subconscious. On the contrary, if you dream during the day while you are awake, you can be assured that you will not only remember this dream of yours but you will have great will power to pursue that dream because you created it in your mind. This type of dreaming lies in the realm of the conscious which makes it closer to our reality. You define the limits and borders of this type of dream and this is why most people who dream like this will put in the work, sweat and tears and will go through the trials and tribulations that are necessary to make those dreams become a reality. These people know for a fact that this is what they truly want for themselves and they will stop for nothing less than the exact vision they have in their heads. Now, they do not chase this dream blindly. They know that it will be hard and they will probably fail on numerous occasions but they keep telling themselves that it is worth it. Usually, what most people don't want to do will have great value to those who are willing to chase them. They know for a fact that if it were easy then everybody would do it. Since most people don't want to do it then it automatically gains importance to those who truly want it and are willing to work for it. They know that eventually their hard work will pay off and they will be happy since they were capable of reaching their goal.

It is no secret that the guy that goes to the gym every single day and actually pushes himself to the limit at the gym day after day feels so good about himself. It is because he is seeing the fruits of his hard labor. What most people see in him is a man that is well built and very strong. What he sees in himself is a man who had a goal that he wanted to reach and went through the difficulties of endless repetitions of heavy weight lifting even though he was exhausted and his muscles were hurting and screaming for mercy. He still kept on going and eventually he got to where he wanted to see himself and he can finally be proud because he has achieved his goal. In the scenario I just described, I hope you realized that hard work go hand in hand with consistency. This means that you need and <u>have to</u> put in the necessary effort in the particular activity on a regular basis in order to reach your personal dream.

It took me four years of going to the gym and literally putting in the time and the energy not only in the weight room but also at home doing research on eating habits that I should have, sleeping habits that I should follow and different workout plans that I tried to finally find what worked for me. With the knowledge that I have acquired, I was capable of consistently putting hard work at the gym and effectively gain the muscle mass that I wanted. What I learned along the way is that you will fail and you will want to give up when the going gets though. But I truly need you to stand your ground and keep on pushing towards that goal because it belongs to you and nobody else.

I found a way to cope with the feeling of wanting to quit due to the difficulty of the task; I set up small goals that I could reach in the near future to get me closer to the bigger picture in my mind. For example, let's say you are going to the gym and you want to have some solid 6 pack abs. I want you to not only focus on visualizing those 6 packs but also on setting up your small goals like flattening the possible belly that you have right now. Once you can do that, you will be one step closer to getting your first set of abs. You need to have small tasks done one after the other and the agglomeration of those tasks will bring forth success. Remember the quote from Jim Rohn that I shared with you in a previous chapter that states that: "Happiness does not come from big pieces of great success, but from small advantages hammered out day by day". You need to focus on achieving small goals every single day because when you put in all those small successes together, you get incredible and unforgettable success.

Look at it this way, it is very easy to break a small twig but the more twigs that you put together and try to break, the harder it gets with each individual twigs that you add to the pile. Translate this teaching here and acknowledge the fact that the first times you will go to the gym, you might fail and break down because your body is not used to this physical stress. If you keep on going and you add the number of days that you endure the hard physical process, the stronger you become and the harder it will be for your spirit to break. You will be telling yourself that you went through this pain already and you know you can surpass it. Whatever trials you are going through during your travel towards your personal goal, stay strong and keep counting the twigs that you add to your basket for each of them will strengthen you more as their numbers grow. Remember the problems you have already faced and that you have surpassed and just keep on pushing.

Edward Balwer Lytton said: "Leave no stone unturned". In other words, you need to give it your all and try every solutions possible. Do not let anything get in your way and just keep pushing and searching until you reach that stone that you will turn only to finally discover your personal success, said success that you have been so valiantly looking for. You will then achieve a level of happiness that most people only dream about in their sleep. You will be able to tell yourself that your hard work has finally paid off. Give yourself a round of applause and now push yourself towards the next level.

CHAPTER 14

CONSISTENCY

To keep up with working hard, it is imperative that I give you key points on maintaining consistency. Hard work does not imply that once one task is taken seriously success will magically incur. When you are working towards reaching your goals, even when you put in hard work in one task, you need to maintain consistency in that task. Remember that you need to have small tasks done one after the other. The combination of each of those tasks will bring forth success for they complement one another. Like I said before, you need to cut up your main goal into multiple smaller and more easily achievable goals that will give you the courage to keep moving forward with every little piece of success that you achieve. The importance of consistency is to make sure that you do not sabotage yourself along the way. I hope that by now you realize that you will face many challenges, some harsher than others, and you will also fail in the presence of some challenges. If you get back up and try again, that is when consistency comes in and plays a huge role into revealing your path.

Do not give up on your goal and keep pushing forward until you succeed. By being consistent and persistent in your actions, you will ensure a greater probability of success and will eventually rise up to the challenge and solve the problem that was presented to you. Les Brown says "reach for the moon and if you fall, try to land on your back because if you can look up, you can get up". You need to be persistent when following your dream. If you fail, get back up and try again. If you fail again, get back up again and keep on trying until you get it right. You need to realise that this is not going to happen tomorrow or in the following week. That is why you need to focus on the present moment with consistency and not worry about the future. When you put in time and energy into completing a specific task at THIS very moment, you cannot afford to start thinking about the unsure future.

You are here at this very moment and are being presented this very opportunity therefore focus on that. However, do keep in mind that only the present is important. Stop focusing on what could possibly happen tomorrow or a month from now because you might not be here a month from now. If you focus on the now, you will leave a legacy that people will remember you for. Don't worry about how it will come to you, just worry on what is happening in the present moment regardless if somebody promised you anything else for the future. Understand that you are not promised with the gift of tomorrow yet thus start working anyway with what you have right now and keep moving forward with great consistency.

With consistency comes a pile-up of tasks that will eventually create adequate skills which will be very useful either alone or as a whole. Unfortunately, if you are not consistent in your actions, you will not develop those skills that will help you win later, on the road to success. Eric Thomas once said that: "if you hit an oak tree a thousand times in a thousand different spots nothing will happen". You might hurt the tree but it will still be standing strong and mighty. Ponder on the rest of the quote though : "If you hit an oak tree a thousand times in the exact same spot over and over again, eventually the tree will fall". Picture your goal at the top of that oak tree and the only way to reach it is to cut the tree down. You will need to consistently hit that tree in the exact same spot over and over again, day by day, until it actually comes down.

Keep in mind that there will be problems that you will have to face. While cutting down a tree, you might get a splinter, you need to make sure that your tools are in good conditions because that tree could be so hard that the axe you use either gets stuck in the tree after a hit or the axe itself shatters under the colossal strength of the tree. You will then need to take a decision. Do I give up and leave my dreams alone and hope that no one else will find them or do I grab a new axe, a better suited axe and start cutting it down again until that tree gives up and crumbles down under the tenacious beatings of the persistent axe? That my friends is the power of consistency and I need you to learn to harvest its power to your benefit. With all the problems that you will have to face, you will develop skills to better your art and said art will start attracting the public's eye during its transition into a better form. Eventually, you will reach a certain point that will permit you to, if you truly want to, educate other people on how to do what you do best.

Ralph Waldo Emerson once said "Life is a succession of lessons which must be lived to be understood". To experience those life lessons, you need to actually go through the multiple problems that life will throw at you. Remember that everyone has problems that they have to face. Nichiren Daishonen wrote "never let life's hardships disturb you … no one can avoid problems, not even sages or saints". To be honest with you, on a fundamental level, we all almost have the same problems, it is our solutions to these problems that make a difference. Most people will try to avoid their problems even though it is impossible to do so. Other people will give up and let the problems get the best of them. Others will give it their all to fix the hard situation that they are facing and keep moving forward until another stressful situation arises. The reason why this is one of the best ways to deal with your problems is because you learn something new even if you fail. If you fail, you need to remain positive, for example you can tell yourself "This is amazing. I just found one way that does not work. So now I know what not to do." You can work on other possibilities from there on out. Change your approach and see if the new mentality works for this situation or not. Jules Renard said it best: "As I grow to understand life lessons, I learn to love it more and more". We have already established that the more you will act towards fulfilling your life dreams the more you will learn, just remember that "commitment leads to action. Action brings your dreams closer" (Marcia Wieder). If you listen to this advice that I am giving you at this very moment and you truly decide to make a commitment not to me, not to your family or friends, not to God but to yourself, you will bring yourself closer to your dream every time you work on the necessary steps. If you are faced with trials on your path, just do what I do and keep repeating this great quote from Isaac Asimov: "Difficulties vanish when faced boldly". Put the chances on your side and give yourself no other option but to find strength to do the necessary work every day that you are blessed with the gift of life.

CHAPTER 15

TIME

I know that we have already addressed this in the beginning of the book, however I want to bring it up again as promised because I believe that now you are ready to go in greater details into this unavoidable concept of time. It is surprising how we take the small things in life for granted every single day. We tend to forget that we are not immortal and that eventually we will die. I believe that we tend to forget because we are afraid of death and avoid thinking about it. The only thing that everyone can be sure of is that eventually, we will all die. Regardless of how everyone dies or when it will happen, the fact remains that we will die. Knowing this, one would think that most people would value their time on this planet and try to utilize it for a greater purpose or cause. Quite the contrary, we tend to spend our time frivolously on minor actions that bring no strong emphasis or change to our lives.

You need to understand what most people will never comprehend until it is too late. Your time is one of the most precious assets that you possess on this earth and yet it is not yours to control. I say this because you cannot control when you will die. When your time comes, you will die regardless of the outcome. If you decided to take your own life, you do not dictate how long your heart will keep on beating and when you will actually take your last breath for example, many people that jump off building or bridges in the hopes to die, land on the ground or water and survive. YOU DO NOT control when you will die.

The most important thing in your arsenal is time because you do not, and will never know how much time you have on this earth. This is where a lot of successful people diverge from most of the population because since they realize that they do not know when they will leave this earth, they try to work every possible moment towards their dreams. Remember what we talked about in the previous time chapter in regards to the mathematical theory of time. There are 24 hours in a day and these 24 hours are shared over the world by everyone. The key point as we discussed, was that nobody really knows if they will have the full 24 hours every single day. I might wake up tomorrow morning at 10am and as I walk out of my house, go through an unexpected situation and die by noon. In that case on my last day, I really only lived for 12 hours. Since no one knows when they will die, you cannot prepare a specific plan to follow until that day comes. What you can do though is start working at this very moment on what you want and see your life as a ticking bomb. Most people who see bombs will just run and thus will not know when the bomb will go off because they cannot see the time. Work as hard as possible to achieve as much as possible until that final unexpected day comes.

We all know that saying, "the early bird gets the worm". Well, I like to take it up a notch and say, not only does "the early bird get the worm", but he has a vast selection of worms to choose from. Once he has made his choice, the next bird to wake up and go after the worms can only choose from what's left. This goes on until the new day arrives and we start over again. If there are no more worms to eat, the first bird is the first to know and can focus his energy into getting the food from somewhere else thus reducing once again the amount left for the next bird. You need to use your time effectively and do this with great speed because you do not know who else is out there chasing the same dream you are chasing. It is your dream and your goal to reach therefore do not let anyone else take what is rightfully yours. If you do not act upon those dreams, you are intentionally giving them away to anyone who is willing to take them. I can guarantee that if you let that happen, you will regret it. Treat your time as the most precious tool that you have because now you know that it does not belong to you.

The other perspective in regards to time that I want to bring up is in regards to the past, the present and the future. On a general basis, people live in the past and always worry about the future. Unconsciously, we tend to block out the present moment continuously. All three are very important and do work together. However, there is a way to manage them in order to fortify their union and maximise your gains from all three. As much as they are all important, the key is to really put 90% of your energy in the present and only 5% on both the past and future.

The past is important because that is where your failures reside. Since you need to learn from your failures, you will need to look in your past and acknowledge what did not work before so that you do not make the same mistakes again. You need to learn from your past and grow from it. Always remember to not let your past bring you down because you cannot change your past, you cannot change the actions that have already taken place and you will have to live with the repercussions of said actions. The amazing thing about the past is that it never really catches up to you unless you allow it to. Regardless of what happened before, you need to understand that you define your future through your past experiences and your present actions.

The future is an unknown territory that you cannot control. Your actions define your future therefore you can try and execute actions that hopefully will lead to desired results but since you never know what can happen, you will never truly know the outcome of a situation completely. This is why you can only afford to spend 5% of your energy and time into the future. That 5% is the time that it will take you to assess the possible outcomes and strive towards what you think is best for you. Once you take a decision on what you truly want to have or accomplish, I will need you to forget about the future and only come back to it when you need to remind yourself of the objective that you are trying to reach.

Now let's talk about the remaining percentage of your attention in regards to the present. There is a reason why I asked you to put in 90% of your energy in the present moment. It is argued that many people have the possibility to either live in the past or live in the future. I personally believe that it is impossible and you should, on the contrary, avoid to follow that erroneous belief. You can chose to focus your time and energy on the past or the POSSIBLE future but you are nonetheless living in the present. Regardless of the action you are undertaking at this very moment, you are living right now at this exact time. Your focus might be in the past or the future but your actions will always remain in the present moment which implies that any decision you have to take will be taken in the present moment.

Think about that 90% now. We are putting great emphasis on the present moment because it is the only time when we can actually make a decision. Those who truly want to be happy must learn to act accordingly. Jim Rohn said that: "Happiness is not something you postpone, it is something you design for the present". The present moment is most important because we can only act now. Each action has an impact on the future but you never truly know what consequences that action will bring. What you must do, is make sure that you know for a fact that the action you decide to go with is truly the one you wanted to take. I like to think about the Latin saying "Carpe Diem" which means in our current terminology: "Enjoy the present day with no worry for tomorrow". Just enjoy your day the best you can and you will be happy. Make sure you concentrate on the present moment because now you know that if your actions are truly those that you desired to take, you will be happy.

Living in the present moment involves taking a lot of actions and decisions. We spoke about this in the chapter covering the decision stage of your path. Remember that if you act the way you want to be, soon you will be the way you act. Your actions define your personality and your personality will dictate your actions. I know it is hard to grasp this concept but if you think about it, you will find the treasure that it holds. Let me share with you how I see it. If you apply it to your life, you will soon realize that the actions that you have been taking have greatly shaped your beliefs and your personality. Afterwards, you need to assess and reflect on yourself to determine if the person you are right now is who you truly want to be. If the answer to that question is yes then keep doing what you are doing. If by any chance the answer is no, ask yourself what actions you need to change to get you where you truly want to be.

The Dalai Lama said: "There are only two days in the year that nothing can be done. One is called yesterday and the other is called tomorrow, so today is the right day to love, believe, live and especially do all you can". Put a lot of time and energy on the present moment and the actions that can be taken at this very moment to ensure your happiness.

CHAPTER 16

FAITH

Let me start off by saying that when I talk about faith, I am in no way referring to, nor restricting to faith in religion. There is a big difference between faith and religion. You can have faith in a religion but you do not need a religion to have faith. You can have faith in yourself, faith in a better future, faith in peace and so on. You can have faith in many things that are not connected to religion. When someone has faith in something, usually the impossible [13] happens. I need you to have unfailing faith in your dreams. Nobody should want this as bad as you want it so no one can have faith in this project more than you. If you start a project with no faith because you are going through some difficult times, how do you expect other people to have faith in it for you? They see the lack of trust that you have in this particular project which will translate in lack of energy spent to make it happen and thus your project is automatically exposed to a high failure rate.

Faith will help you through each and every step that you will have to go through, especially those that will be the hardest. This is why having faith is so important. Like I told you before, you will fail and it will be hard but with faith, you will get back up and try again because you truly believe that this will work for you. Faith is an important stepping stone that leads to success and I believe that you should put it as the first stepping stone when you fall. Faith should be the hand helping you back up when you fall down. The key point here is for you to know that you need more than one stepping stone to reach the other side of the river. We have been working on a couple of them since the beginning of this book without

---

[13]   Impossible: Due to lack of wording I had to use impossible but remember that not much in this world is impossible

you realising it and now, if you look back and see what you have accomplished you should be proud of yourself for getting this far. Don't you truly believe that you should have faith in yourself especially after all that you have changed in your life for yourself? Have faith in yourself and your talent but most importantly have faith in all the skills that you have developed from the beginning of this special journey that you decided to go on.

Once your faith is strong enough, you will meet people who believe in you and in your personal project. You will find people who can help you with their talents and you can help them with yours. Help each other out and push each other towards your respective end goals. It is important that you control your entourage because your entourage will unfortunately influence your path. The people that you hang out with is a great way for you to assess the activities that you undertake in your life. You sometimes hear that "Birds of a feather flock together". If you are trying to become a professional athlete, you should try your best to find people who have succeeded in that field and learn from them. It would also greatly help you to find yourself a coach who will train you and push you to your limits at every practice. Your entourage will be beneficial for your dream; have faith in their knowledge and skills to help you grow and better yourself. There is a French song that I like a lot that illustrates this. For those who don't read French, I will translate it afterwards but the poetic genius of the song needs to be maintained for my French readers.

> *"Les yeux baissés, les mains tendues au ciel*
> *Où est la foi j'aurais tant besoin d'elle*
> *À l'approche de la fin les gens s'aident*
> *On se rapproche quand les galères s'enchaînent"*
>
> *La Fouine / Musique : Vécue*

> *"Eyes closed, hands towards the sky,*
> *Where is the faith for I would need it?*
> *When the end comes close, people help each other out,*
> *For we tend to get closer to our neighbors when the problems follow one another"*
>
> *La Fouine / Musique : Vécue*

This song symbolises the effect that faith has on situations. Think about all the things that you did when you unknowingly had faith in yourself. Also think of when other people had faith in you which made you have even more faith in yourself. When that happened, didn't you feel the energy flow through you? Did you use that energy to get the wanted results? People who have faith in you will help you out the best way they can and therefore, your path, which you have been creating for yourself, is now shared with different people who are there to lift you up when you fall or give you the tools to help you create that path faster. Always make sure that your faith is stronger than your fears. It is good to have fears but the faith that you show to confront that fear and beat it should be stronger than the fear itself. As much as fear is useful, it should never control your movements. Have faith in yourself and keep moving forward even though you do not see the end of the tunnel.

CHAPTER 17

RISK

When talking about risk, you cannot eliminate the importance of faith which is why I presented the concept of faith beforehand. Taking risks is very crucial to your path for, those risks will bring you to the next stepping stone. Think about all the successful people in life, they took huge risks in their lives to pursue the goal that they had so much faith in. In one of his teachings, Les Brown said: "If you are not willing to risk, you cannot grow, if you cannot grow, you cannot be your best, if you cannot be your best, you cannot be happy and if you cannot be happy then what else is there."

Let's focus on the first part of the sentence "If you are not willing to risk, you cannot grow". When he says that, he is expressing the importance of risk for one's personal advancement. Think about where you are in life and think about all the decisions you took to get there. Each and every one of those decisions are risks that you took. This is why we can say that your present life is the combination of many consequences[14] and/or results that were made possible because of those risks. I created a small diagram that illustrate the cycle that happens on a daily basis.

---

[14] Consequence: Keep in mind that a consequence is not always negative. The definition of consequence is a direct or indirect result or effect of an action or condition.

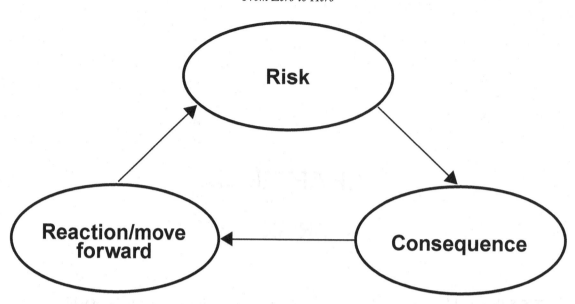

This becomes the cycle of everyday living. Every day, you are called to take small decisions that will have a tremendous impact on your near and long term future. Most people don't realize that getting out of bed is in itself a risk that automatically brings consequences. The fact that you got out of bed at 6 am and you were ready at 7 am might be one of the reason why you might potentially miss the morning rush/traffic and get to work earlier than someone who woke up at 6:05 am. I can guarantee that leaving your house 5 minutes later can make a big difference in regards to morning traffic and thus illustrates the functioning of risk.

When taking risks, as much as it could be a good thing to think about the situation and the potential consequences, try your best not to ponder too much on the possible results. One thing that you should know by now is that you can never know what will happen. Once you have evaluated the situation and thought of a couple of possible results, just take action and accept the true resulting consequences. There is a special saying that I love to follow when I have to take major decisions and it is the basis of this book and the reason why this book even exists.

"Thinking is in the realm of the brain, doing is in the realm of the heart"
author unknown.

Usually when you think, you mostly think of the negative results that can happen and, since most people do not want to get hurt, they will not act due to fear. If you do not control your thoughts, then you are letting fear govern your life and you will not be able to succeed.

I need you to trust in yourself and just take the risk. If you stop for a second and think, I can guarantee that you will never be able to find all the possible consequences that might come to life but what you might find is that one action that truly belongs to your heart. Stop trying to think of all the possible consequences and just act. Remember that what you will envision is usually anything but a fraction of what could truly happen. Take for example an iceberg; when you look at an iceberg and you want to avoid it, you logically start calculating the size of the ship and the size of the iceberg that you are seeing on your path. Here is the problem though with the iceberg, most of it is hidden underwater and unfortunately, you do not see the hidden part. You could take all the time to calculate all you want, you could still end up hitting it because you were so focused on what you were seeing that you did not pay attention to your sonar system (heart in our cases as human beings) that is leading you and telling you where the danger is. Take the risk of following your heart and let it guide you around the iceberg until you get to safety for only the heart truly knows not only what will bring you happiness but what road to take to get you there.

CHAPTER 18

GOALS

You should be extremely happy with your progress so far because not only have you been working hard towards something that you really want, but I know that some of you are getting discouraged right about now. The amazing thing though is that you are still hoping that your dreams will come true which will give you the strength to keep on pushing. There is a great exercise that you can practice to help you not only get through but also prevent future discouragements. It is very simple to do: set yourself some goals. Now for this to work, you must make sure that it is done right and diligently. The first thing you need to make sure that you do when setting yourself goals, is to make sure you write them down. Once you write them down, you limit the chances of forgetting them. I will ask that you keep them somewhere that is within your eyesight every day (in the morning for maximum success rate). By seeing them every day, you will be reminded to keep pushing until that goal is reached.

There is a huge mistake that I want you to avoid for the consequences to it can be dire. The mistake that you can make is to have found the ultimate goal that you are striving for and keep that in mind. As much as that is acceptable, it is important that you set yourself some intermediate goals towards that ultimate goal. In other words, you need to accomplish each subsidiary goal in the order that you have put them in. This creates small attainable actions that will bring the feeling of success and progression each and every time you achieve one of them until you get to the ultimate goal. With each small goal you achieve, the more confident you will become and you will haste to work towards the next small goal. You will keep on pushing because you know that since you got to this small goal, you will get to others as well. To make things even easier for yourself, regroup a certain quantity of small goals into a category that can be represented by a medium goal. This means that when you have achieved for example 5 small goals, you know that you just completed your first intermediate goal which implies that you are closer to the end zone.

Here is the downfall that I need you to work on and watch out for right now. I need you to avoid self-destructive ideas and perceptions about your goals. You need to understand that you will subconsciously try to discourage yourself from achieving the smallest task possible. Now the reason why you have to focus on a small task individually is because if you do fail, you can rest assured that you will be able to get back on your feet and try again because failing the small task will not affect you as much as failing the biggest one will. People have a specific way of thinking about themselves in a negative way that will only demoralize them. You need to remember that this was just a small task and that you can complete it if you truly work hard and dedicate yourself towards crossing that task off your list. Remember that as a living being, you are powerful and therefore you should act and be powerful.

You have the intellectual potential to do so much yet you tend to do so little. Let me give you a small anecdote that I used to hear a lot when I was younger. In Haiti, where I come from, people used to say that if you ask a man to jump a wall that is twice his size, he will tell you that he cannot do it and therefore he will give up without even trying. They would proceed by saying that if a dog would be chasing that same man, he will unknowingly at least try to jump that wall to save his life. Surprisingly enough the man will most of the time go over the wall. The key point here is that they at least tried to jump the wall and whether they succeed or not, they have accomplished way more than in the first scenario. Now, picture me talking to you at this very moment and asking you : Why don't you try your best to jump as high as possible right now instead of waiting for that dog to come along not knowing if it actually will catch up with you or not. Jump and see if you cannot get over that wall. Now imagine that your goal is hidden behind that wall and all you have to do is work hard until you can jump over that wall and finally lay your hands on the goal that you have been dreaming of for so long. Why don't you start working hard at this very moment to get that well deserved reward as fast as you can? You have nothing to lose right now if you try so NOW is the perfect moment to start working on getting that dream that you so desperately want. The time is not tomorrow and not in two hours, it is now and only now for now is the only certainty that we have in life.

The next thing I need you to work on is to stop selling yourself short. I know of so many people who are quick to say that they are not as good of a singer as their favorite singers, or other people who say that they would love to be as fit as their friend but they cannot follow the same workout routine or wake up that early. I used to be one of those people and I used to spit out those same excuses. Just to show you, here is an excuse I used to repeat to myself every single day: I cannot get stronger because my genetics won't allow it, or because I love eating fast food too much or because I hate exercising and it hurts or even because it is so hard. The list of excuses that I was capable of finding to not go to the gym became so long that I started to get tired of remembering all of them. My mentality changed when I discovered motivational videos and I learned one of the greatest lessons of my life. When other people are in horrible life situations, with no clear road to success, find a way to succeed. You should take that as an example that you can also make it happen for you. Don't try to duplicate what they are doing. Learn from their mistakes and make your own path by pushing through the struggles until you succeed.

When you make up your mind, there is not much that you cannot achieve. That is why I made up my mind and decided that I would wake up every morning at 6 am and go to the gym. It was hard at first but I gave myself some small weight and size goals that I wanted to achieve in a set amount of time. With the right actions taken and the energy that I put in day by day, I started seeing result after result and eventually it became a habit for me to achieve my small term goals that brought me closer to my bigger, more important goals. I had to learn the hard way that I shouldn't compare myself to others but only acquire knowledge from their experiences. Listen to me, you can admire their success, but you need to analyze their mistakes and listen to their suggestions in order to gain their knowledge. In the end, you need to do what I did, you need to put your ideas and your opinion in writing to make this work for you the way YOU perceive it. This is something that you WANT and you know HOW you want it therefore input your personal touch and adapt it to your particular lifestyle. If a famous basketball player says that every day he used to make 500 shots, why don't you go out there and make 700 shots just to make it harder on yourself. If you truly want to have what he has or even more than what he has, push it even further and add some push-ups for each single shot that you miss. You will suffer along the way but, not only will you get stronger physically, you will also master your shots. Your body movements will synchronise and your precision will greatly improve to avoid having to do more push ups. In other words, you will not want to do push ups at some point and will force yourself to get those 700 shots in the basket without missing a single one. You will at that point, surpass the one that you have idolized for so long and you will feel glorious, strong and confident that you can do more to better yourself. Just keep trying your best to check off all the small/short term goals that you have and they will strengthen you so you can get the bigger picture achieved on the long run. Surpass your limits and grow with each new experience. The knowledge will be priceless and the results will be epic. Achieve your desired greatness for only you can take yourself there.

CHAPTER 19

SUCCESS/FAILURE

From a very young age I used to tell myself that I never wanted to fail. I always wanted to succeed and never fail at anything. I am very grateful to have learn very fast that failure and success are strongly connected. You cannot have one without the other. To reach success, you will have to go through failure. It is only fair enough that I start talking about the one that is to my point of view the most important. Failure for me is the most important one of the two. If you really want to be successful, you need to make sure that you prepare yourself mentally to go through any failure that is necessary and very often unavoidable.

Let me demonstrate why I think that failure is more important. Be honest with yourself now and ponder on this for a second, why do you think you appreciate light so much? The only reason why you are thankful for the light that shines is because you know how uncomfortable the darkness is. Once you go through darkness and suffer by learning to deal with the hard situations that hide in darkness, you will work hard to make sure that light will always be available for you to see and thus prepare for the other possible hard times that might be waiting for you in the near future. What you have to understand here is that you need to be comfortable in the dark because if you are, just imagine what you can do when you are presented with light. I have to use that quote from The Dark Knight movie again because it illustrates this point with such precision and accuracy. Bane says: "Batman you adopted to the dark, I was born in the dark, molded by it, I didn't see the light before I was already a man". Use the darkness to your advantage because in darkness, you will fail and by failing, you will learn in advance how to deal with so many situations which will be helpful later on when the opportunity presents itself.

"It is better to be prepared for an opportunity and not have one than to have an opportunity and not be prepared." (Whitney M. Young Jr.)The reason why the path to success needs failure is because if failure was not present, you would take your success for granted. With failure, you will be able to remember the pain that you went through that got you where you are right now. That pain will push you and motivate you to keep the status that you have <u>rightfully</u> acquired. You will be ready to face the new opportunities that will be presented to you soon. Only then will you know the value of what you possess. With such knowledge, you will be able to multiply your assets to ensure their survival during your lifetime and only then will you realize that the greatest success is not what you possess as material assets but what you have learned along the way that helped you get what you wanted. Remember that no one can take knowledge away from you. You might own 20 cars and they might get destroyed in one day but the knowledge that you have is yours to own. With that knowledge, you will be able to get 20 more cars again to replace the old ones. This is one of the biggest reasons why I have been saying since the beginning that your success does not and should never stop at money or cars or houses or any other material possessions for that matter.

It is a known fact that material assets come and go but knowledge is power. That power, once acquired, is very hard to get rid of. Your success is permanent because your knowledge is yours to keep until the end of time. Now, since you know how to get that power, you need to go through the dark times and acquire bits and pieces of knowledge along the way, keep telling yourself that success is a quiet daily set of tasks that you do over and over again until you become an expert at them. Remember that you will need to work on your dream using your personal skills and in time people will give you the necessary push to propel you forward. I need you to remember that it has to start within you and you should never wait on anybody to go after what you want. Take the first step and do it for yourself because you are the one who truly wants this for yourself. I have tried to tell you that it will take time and it will take a great amount of energy but it will all be worth it especially when you start seeing little results daily. The beauty of it is that when you analyze your habits to see the changes that occurred since the beginning, you will not see small changes. On the contrary, you will witness enormous changes which entitle great results that you will be proud of because it all came from your efforts. It is very funny to see how we do not realize how different we are from yesterday but if you look back a couple of months, if not years, you see huge differences. That is the power of day to day actions. At that point, you will be your biggest fan, your biggest ally but most importantly, your biggest accomplishment until you go after another piece of the cake.

CHAPTER 20

REVENGE/CONCLUSION

I need you to pay great attention here because it is easy to misinterpret and misuse this concept. If you do not take the time to grasp the intensity of this concept, it can have a massive negative impact on your journey. Revenge here is attached, from my point of view, to success. Now, be warned that I am not saying that you need to go and get revenge nor am I using this term in a derogatory way. When I talk about revenge, I am referring to the moment in your journey when you have reached success. Your revenge will come to you in the following way: along your path, you will have many people who will try to discourage you, bring you down and make you feel stupid and inadequate in this struggle that you have decided to go through that we have labeled as your personal pursuit of your happiness. The revenge that I am referring to happens when those same people will now come to you and ask you about your journey once you become successful. They will want to know how you achieved success and you will get revenge not by shutting them down or laughing in their faces. On the contrary, you get revenge by actually taking them under your wing and sharing your knowledge with them. You are now in a position to help them get to where they want to be because you know what you went through and what you had to do along the way. Help them fight their demons and get where they want to be. Show them that you know the power of self-confidence and the importance of believing in yourself to achieve your goals in life. Show them that even though they did not believe in themselves before, it is not too late to change that mentality. You did it by yourself, so imagine the happiness that you will get to help them get it as well.

Frank Sinatra said that "the best revenge is massive success" because at that point in your life, you will have proved, to everyone that did not believe in you and who gave up on your objective and vision, that it was not only possible, but that you did it and you succeeded. You have done what all of them told you that you could never do in your life. You have showed them that when you truly want something and if you put in the necessary work, you will get what you deserve. This is how you get revenge. It will feel great to know that your hard work and your persistence allowed you to get to where you wanted to be. Naysayers will be at your feet asking you how you did it. Your job now will be to share that knowledge for the profit of others and help them towards their personal achievements.

The struggle is hard but the reward is just sweet. I would say, even sweeter than the sweetest nectar. Remember what you went through to keep the euphoric feeling flowing through your thoughts. Now that you have achieved the level of happiness that you have searched for, keep in mind that perfection doesn't exist which means that you can always better yourself. Go through all the steps over again, and become a greater practitioner than you were before. There are some steps through which you might not need to go again because you have mastered them. Nonetheless, it is always good to have a reminder as to not forget the important lessons that you learned from those theories. You need to make sure that those theories become a part of your everyday life. Trust me, it is easier said than done but you know for a fact that there is nothing in life that is easy. As much as it is not easy, it is worth it. Even if failure is complicated and hurtful, the thing that most people don't know is that if you actually put in work, even when you go through failure, you will learn and achieve success. Make sure you chose the right actions in order to move towards your success and keep visualizing what you are not now for what you are going to be. You could be rich and yet still not have the family that you want. The only thing you can do here is to keep imagining that family in your mind and go after it for you know that deep inside, you truly deserve to have that family. Just keep pushing, work hard and you will go from being a ZERO to a HERO and that my friend is a promise I make to you if you promise me and promise yourself that you will work hard and take all the steps seriously. Put in action and rejoice in your victory. This is your day, it is your time to shine so go out there show the world what you are capable of accomplishing. Better yet, prove yourself wrong by working twice as hard as you think you can work and shine as bright as you can. You are a super star and an incredible being with tremendous powers. Use those powers and make your dreams come true. My friend at this very moment, you no longer are the NOBODY that others picture but instead you are the HERO that you see and materialize daily. Go after your dreams.

NOTES

Chapter 1
    Brain storming ideas

Chapter 2
    Transcript and arrange ideas
    Decisions/roads to take

Chapter 7
    Your why
    (3 lines to input your why)

Chapter 8
    Define and write down values good or bad

Chap 18
    Write final goal
    Write medium goals
    Write smaller goals (under medium)

REFERENCES

Most of the quotes that I used here were found about 5 years ago which is why I do not have the exact location I found them. I have a good habit of writing things that I like down on my personal notebook in case I might need it in the future. I have unfortunately not taken the habit of writing down where the quote came from. I can only elude to some of them through the motivational videos that I have watched throughout the years. I still give credit to the authors when I am aware of the authors. To those authors that recognizes their quotes and I put Unknown author, I apologize and thank you as well for your contribution to this world. If I used a quote from you, it means that some way or another you have affected my life for the best.

QUOTES

It is our light not our darkness that most frightens us Our
deepest fear is not that we are inadequate.
Our deepest fear is that we are powerful beyond measure.
It is our light not our darkness that most frightens us.
—Marianne Williamson

Les brown books and motivational speeches
Eric Thomas motivational speeches
Jim Rohn motivational speeches
The Dark Knight Rises movie (2012)